THE DESERT HAWKS

THE
DESERT HAWKS

Leo Nomis with Brian Cull

GRUB STREET · LONDON

Published by
Grub Street
The Basement
10 Chivalry Road
London SW11 1HT

A catalogue record is available on request from the British Library

ISBN 1-898697-82-5

Typeset by Pearl Graphics, Hemel Hempstead

Printed and bound in Great Britain by
Biddles Ltd, Guildford and King's Lynn

CONTENTS

ACKNOWLEDGEMENTS

Brian Cull wishes to thank his wife Val for her invaluable support during the preparation of this book, which entailed much editing and re-typing. He also thanks his friend and fellow author Shlomo Aloni for supplying additional information and photographs, as he does Frederick Galea, Hon Secretary of the National War Museum Association of Malta and long-standing friend, who also supplied some photographs.

Despite poor health, Leo Nomis has gamely continued to embellish his original account with additional anecdotes.

We both congratulate artist Chris Thomas for his excellent dustjacket illustration, and we thank our publisher, John Davies of Grub Street, for this first-class production.

INTRODUCTION

FROM FLEDGLING EAGLE TO FIGHTER PILOT

I was born [on 9 March 1922] and educated in the Los Angeles area of California, where the usually mild weather permitted sport flying the entire year. My father, after whom I was named, had qualified as a pilot with the US Air Service in 1917 but was held back as an instructor on Curtiss JN4s at Kelly Field, Texas. Before he could apply for overseas duty he was involved in a serious crash which killed the student and put my father in hospital until after the Armistice in 1918. He was discharged the following year as a Captain. He became a Hollywood stuntman and was killed in 1932 while performing aerobatics. I do believe he had influence on my decision later to fly myself, although I never flew with him. I had early on learned the primary elements of aviation by frequenting the airports on the outskirts of the city and obtaining odd jobs for which I would be rewarded with flying time. During the summer of 1940 I logged a certain amount of solo hours in this manner.

By the end of 1940, a growing number of American volunteers were being attracted into Royal Air Force service in spite of the US official status of neutrality. Many others had already actively entered into the war through the Canadian forces and, in the spring of 1941, by British-American accord, several training fields had been established in the United States specifically to prepare American pilots for duty with the RAF. Though the British Government had obvious political reasons behind creating these contingent bases in the US, the move expedited the enlistment of scores of American pilots who had hitherto been delayed in their quest to fight a foreign war. The requirements for acceptance into what became known as the Clayton Knight contingents were considered lenient and a total of 75 flying hours was the standard minimum for the applicants. Some who entered upon the adventure, however, had much less previous flight experience than the suggested quota.

Although experienced on only light aircraft of the era, I had, by the beginning of 1941, been accepted into one of the RAF training courses at Glendale, California. After a three-month interval in which we were instilled, by civilian instructors, with the principles and procedures of basic and advanced flight techniques on Harvard trainers, I left for Ottawa, Canada with a group of ten others. We were all young, some being under 20 years of age, and like most emerging pilots of that time we were looking for action with no serious idea of the grim realities that lay ahead. I think all of us, with very few exceptions, were simply adventurers and romanticists, and perhaps idealists. Few were patriots, but it probably worked into that later for those who got a real taste of what the war was, and who were permitted the chance to view liberty from a distance. Most of us had a vague conviction that America would eventually enter the obviously worsening conflict and we rationalized that we were merely getting a head start. It turned out, in essence, that this over-simplified reason for volunteering was to become perfectly true.

In Ottawa, though technically civilians, we were commissioned Pilot Officers in the RAF Volunteer Reserve at the British Liaison Office in Government Building. We did not receive our uniforms until we arrived in London three weeks later. A preview of what the future held was presented to us that August of 1941 when we were shipped out of Halifax, Nova Scotia on a North Atlantic convoy. Within a week we were witness to the sinking of several ships by German U-boats. Three of the American group were missing presumed killed in this attack.

Our arrival in Britain was heralded by an air raid and on our first evening in London we were rapidly becoming aware that we were in a war. However, the excitement of being in England rekindled our spirits and within two days we were sent to 56 Operational Training Unit at Sutton Bridge in Lincolnshire. Our position at the time was rather unique because, although we were already commissioned officers in the Royal Air Force, we had yet to endure any actual training under the British code of discipline and the OTU at which we arrived was to be our first encounter with this delight. Our closest association with British military rules to this point had been when we pledged obedience to the King's Rules and Regulations, a document whose contents were completely unfamiliar to us at the time.

At the airfield we were fascinated with the countryside and strange customs, and we were anxious to get into the air again. This desire was not long denied us. The first day we were checked out in the Miles Master advanced trainers by seemingly bored Battle of Britain veterans, and within a week we were airborne in Hurricane Is which, too, had been through the Battle of Britain. Summer was ending but the weather was good and with the flat checker-board terrain spread away beneath the wings of the aircraft, life seemed marvellous indeed. The instruments and controls of the British machines were strange to us at first but we soon learned to master the illustrious hump-back fighters, although the accident and fatality rate at the OTU was alarmingly high. Like most who finally face war close up we seemed to develop the fatalistic point of view that we personally were not going to die in the debacle and so we treated it as a huge and precarious game. This mental adjustment, however, did not prevent each day from providing a certain amount of apprehension and anxiety.

As the autumn of 1941 approached and the clouds and fog were increasing above the Midlands, we completed the six-week course and were, in a loose sense, certified as fighter pilots. We were forthwith posted to operational units and I found myself, along with one of the other Americans, assigned to 71 (Eagle) Squadron. After a two-day leave in London's West End, which apparently was the meeting place for all services in those days, we boarded the train out of Victoria Station for RAF North Weald in nearby Essex. There was probably not another city quite like London in the war. The bombings and the blackout did nothing to restrict the revelry that the masses performed on a nightly basis, as if it were the last chance for hilarity and companionship. The Regent Palace Bar was probably the single most popular spot for the cast of thousands who then passed that way. An officers' bar, this was to become the general headquarters for most Eagle Squadron members when on leave.

Our blue dress uniforms still had the appearance of newness and when the train stopped at the North Weald station we were in high spirits because 71 Squadron was in the RAF's famous 11 Group, from whence most of the offensive sorties over enemy territory were being launched. We thought we were ready for action. 71 Squadron was the first of the three units in the RAF which were composed entirely of American volunteer pilots, and it was to achieve the distinction of being the highest scoring squadron in 11 Group for the month of October that year.

Our quarters were comfortable at North Weald and within a week we went on operations, though it was first necessary to be checked out on the Spitfire V which the Squadron was operating. The Spitfire was quite different from the Hurricane in many ways but we were soon assigned to convoy patrol duty [first operational flight in AB812 on 7 December 1941], which at best was a monotonous task where our worst enemy was the weather. However, it gave us the opportunity to become acquainted with the remarkable capabilities of the Spitfire and if the weather seemed bad that autumn, the devastating winter – which would be recorded as the most severe in two decades – was fast arriving. The fighter sweeps and bomber escort missions over enemy-held France that had occupied the summer and autumn months were cancelled because of the weather. The dangerous low-level sorties known as Rhubarbs were still authorised periodically as volunteer missions but the Wing activities that winter were sharply curtailed by Group Operations. The Rhubarbs, however, could always be counted on to provide unlimited excitement or tragedy, or both. The CO of 71 Squadron, Sqn Ldr Chesley Peterson, was an excellent leader and at 23 was the first American Squadron Leader in the RAF. Not a high-scoring ace by other standards, he was nevertheless an exceptional pilot and was to lead well over 100 missions before the Eagles were disbanded. His job was none the easier when the first snow fell. The pilot quality in 71 Squadron was basically good, including several pilots with exceptional potential, but the Eagles were conspicuous by the fact that they did not produce any really high scoring aces, though several were to reach this plateau while serving later with other squadrons.

When America entered the war there were rumors that we would be immediately transferred to the US Command. This theory proved to be laughably premature. American forces were, at that time, far from being ready for any actual operations in Europe and it was to be ten long months before the Eagle Squadrons as a unit would be absorbed into the USAAF as the 4th Fighter Group. The majority of Americans who served with RAF or Dominion air forces did not necessarily see duty with the Eagle Squadrons, but were in reality scattered among the many and diverse units and commands of the day. Most of these had transferred to US authority by the summer of 1943 but a few served out the entire war with British squadrons. Some who were with the Eagles at one time or another were posted out east – the Mediterranean or Middle East – before the mass transfer of the following autumn was effected.

Meanwhile, losses due to weather, accidents and Rhubarbs began to mount as we sat out that winter at RAF Martlesham Heath in Suffolk [to where 71 Squadron had moved], and when spring came around in the fateful year of 1942 we had learned that flying was no longer just fun. It was duty, survival and oft-times fear. At any rate the actions of the Eagle Squadrons during that first winter were forgiveably unillustrious, although 71 Squadron had, in January 1942, one of the first real encounters with the Luftwaffe's newly introduced FW190 which was rapidly replacing the Messerschmitt 109 on the Western Front.

If one remained at the Squadron for several months one was assigned a personal aircraft and by April I had acquired a Spitfire [BL287 XR-C] which I rather adolescently adorned with a Red Indian head to signify that I was, to a certain degree, of Sioux Indian ancestry. My father, born in 1889 in Indiana, was one half Irish and one half Sioux Indian [inevitably, due to this ancestry, Leo was known to his colleagues in 71 Squadron as The Chief]. I had an accident with my new machine a short time later during a high wind.

During this period [on 17 April 1942] I was involved in an interception of a Ju88 which had made a hit and run attack on a convoy east of the Suffolk town of Felixstowe. My companion, JJ Lynch, attacked from dead astern. I saw black smoke coming out of Lynch's engine and he pulled away to port, saying on the R/T that he had been hit*. Again I closed in, firing, until the bomber suddenly reared on its tail, hung quivering for a moment, then whipped over and dived straight into the sea. My own aircraft [BL287 XR-C] was hit but I just managed to return to Martlesham Heath with an almost empty tank [Leo had, in fact, opened his account a few weeks earlier while flying AB907 when, on 11 January 1942, he engaged a Ju88 off Lowestoft which he damaged before it managed to escape in the prevailing murky conditions: see Appendix I].

By April the large fighter sweeps resumed over the continent and 71 Squadron moved from Martlesham Heath to RAF Debden in Essex, and became part of 153 Wing. An interesting sidenote on this particular RAF Wing was that in July 1942 it was actually scheduled, as a token force, to go to Russia and participate jointly with the Soviet Air Force at the Battle of Stalingrad. The move had to be cancelled when the preceding convoy to Murmansk, which carried Spitfire IXs for the entire Wing, was almost totally destroyed on the run past Norway. There is no way to contemplate what might have happened or how different everything might have been had we gone out there that terrible year.

Fighter sweeps increased with the arrival of summer and varied with the whims of Fighter Command Operations. All of the squadrons in 11 Group were involved and Spitfires were generally employed in a bomber escort role or simply for fighter attrition. The German High Command was understandably preoccupied at this stage with the enormous campaign on the Eastern Front and the Luftwaffe force in the West was primarily relegated to defense squadrons which, although comparatively thin, were of a high quality as far as veteran flying personnel was concerned, and were unrelenting in their aggressiveness against the RAF strike missions. One of these German units in particular became quite familiar to us at the time and was known for the remainder of the war as the 'Abbeville Boys' [this was the Messerschmitt Bf109-equipped Jadgeschwader 26, based at Abbeville, south of Le Touquet on the Channel coast].

I, among others, was intrigued, somewhat naively, by the reported actions at Malta and in the Western Desert. I volunteered for an overseas posting at the end of July, along with another 71 Squadron pilot, Plt Off Art Roscoe, and received orders to report to Glasgow in Scotland. We said farewell to the Eagle Squadron and the same evening were on a train north. We had no idea of our new destination until after we boarded the aircraft carrier HMS *Furious* with the rest of the overseas contingent at Glasgow and were notified that we would be proceeding to Malta. The *Furious,* which was anchored in the Clyde, was to transport us to a point

---

* Leo's companion, Plt Off John Lynch, managed to reach the coast where he crash-landed his damaged aircraft, suffering facial injuries. Lynch was later posted to Malta where he commanded 249 Squadron, gaining the DFC and Bar for ten victories plus a further seven shared.

in the Mediterranean from where the new Spitfire Vs, which were stowed below decks, would take us on the final leg to the besieged island. It was the beginning of another part of the war for us, and was to be accompanied by hardships we had not been exposed to in England. *Furious* was a short-decked carrier which catered normally to Swordfish and Albacore biplane torpedo-bombers, and there was some concern about the Spitfires having enough running room to get off the flight deck, a theoretical problem that was soon solved by fitting the fighters with the powerful but sometimes faulty hydromatic propellers.

The carrier glided down the Clyde and quietly out to sea on the afternoon of 5 August 1942, escorted by the heavy cruiser HMS *Manchester*, and we felt a certain homesickness at leaving the UK and travelling once more toward the unknown. The group of 20 pilots [there were, in fact, 38 pilots aboard *Furious*] included the usual mixture of British and Commonwealth ranks and, as we headed south through the Irish Sea, we began temporarily to adopt the Navy life. By coincidence, the senior officer in the flight party was Grp Capt Churchill, who had been the first leader of the infant 71 Squadron in the waning days of 1940. Churchill, an excellent officer and personally a fine gentleman, was en route to a base commander assignment at Malta and would take the first section off the *Furious*. With only the company of the *Manchester* on the vast expanse of sea we continued southward without incident and three days later rendezvoused at Gibraltar with an awesome array of ships. The Malta convoy was codenamed Operation Pedestal, and in later years historians of World War II would connect its role in the relief of Malta to the major Axis setbacks in both the Mediterranean and North Africa.

On the night of 9 August the convoy slipped out of the shelter of Gibraltar and when the sun rose on the clear morning of the 10th, the spectacle which became visible in the early light was, in effect, extraordinary. The score of merchant vessels which were bound for the distant island fortress were in the center of an armada of fighting vessels, among which were five aircraft carriers including the US Navy's *Wasp*, two battleships, the *Rodney* and the *Nelson*, and untold numbers of outlying cruisers and destroyers. Oddly enough, the only participants in this famous flotilla who were actually supposed to land at Malta were the merchantmen and the Spitfires from *Furious*. Because of exposure to enemy air attacks, which could be hurled forth incessantly from bases on Sardinia and Sicily, the bulk of the powerful Navy escort would begin turning back for Gibraltar at the midway point of this perilous voyage. At the time, we Spitfire pilots knew nothing of the strategy and were aware only of our own departure hour and air route. As we settled into our cockpits, German high-level bombers were actually in the sky directly above us. The *Rodney*, which was close by the *Furious* at that moment, nearly blacked out the noontime sun with bursts from its anti-aircraft guns. Then, shortly before the third section was due off the windswept flight deck, the convoy came under a determined attack by U-boats and, as I lifted from the *Furious* in my Spitfire [EP410], four torpedoes struck the port side of HMS *Eagle* and, by the time we had formed the flight above the now-harassed convoy, the stricken carrier had disappeared beneath the blue surface of the sea.

Others ships, including the *Manchester*, were to sink that day in the same attack and, of the merchant freighters and tankers, only half would survive the next three days to dock in Grand Harbor at Valetta. We, however, were soon away from the unsettling scene at 20,000 feet, paralleling the seemingly peaceful coasts of Algeria and Tunisia until we cut across Cap Bon eastward to where the waiting island lay. Using most of our fuel, which included 90 gallons in external belly tanks, we landed on the main airfield at Luqa at four o'clock in the afternoon.

Two or three minutes after landing on Malta, we began to entertain the thought that we had made a mistake in applying for an overseas posting. Fate had, nevertheless, decreed it and here we would stay until we departed, one way or another. It was a thought that was not particularly aided in its absence of tranquility by the words of a suntanned and wild-looking Wing Commander who informed us, before we had hardly emerged from our cockpits, that 'you have two weeks to live!' This grim and unkind estimate of our remaining life span was based on a current theory that the average length of a fighter pilot's existence at Malta was a fortnight. Surrounded by a visible atmosphere of death on that small white island, with its incongruous surplus of churches and blasted stonework in the middle of the sea, we believed him. It turned out that for many who were there that day his statement was surprisingly accurate*.

Malta. All who served there would never forget it. They should have awarded a medal for merely arriving at Malta. I have never been to another place with such an atmosphere of doom, violence and toughness about it at first sight. Coming out from England as we did, the filth, flies, diseases and near starvation absolutely fascinated us, the more so because the interception missions were not in the least deterred by these handicaps. It was oppressive, it was in many ways a daily tragedy, one was always hungry – one tin of bully beef and two pieces of stale bread per day, sometimes supplemented by incredibly tasteless local vegetables. The tiresome repetition of this diet was almost as hard to endure as the shortage itself. One was often ill and almost everyone went a little crazy out there. It was a solitary British bastion between Gibraltar and Alexandria and its torpedo-bombers and MTBs were the only

---

* Of the 37 pilots who accompanied Leo to Malta from the *Furious*, nine would be killed in action within a few weeks including Grp Capt Churchill, one taken prisoner and four wounded. Among the latter was his American friend, Art Roscoe (see *Malta: The Spitfire Year, 1942* by Chris Shores, Brian Cull and Nico Malizia, published by Grub Street).

obstacle in the path of Rommel's supply line to Libya. The island refused to die. It was the only piece of land in the war to be awarded a medal (the George Cross) and it was to be acclaimed as the most bombed section of earth in the world. The Spitfires, nightfighters and anti-aircraft batteries were its sole defense and the Luftwaffe and Italians continued to pressure the island with admirable persistency. Their failure to neutralize Malta totally, however, was ultimately to be a significant factor in the Axis defeat in North Africa.

On the second day I was assigned to 229 Squadron which was stationed at Takali in the north-eastern sector. The other unit on this airfield was 249 (Gold Coast) Squadron, whose membership boasted the presence of George Beurling, a Canadian who was proving to be a phenomenal air fighter. During heavy enemy activity we were scrambled six times a day at this base, and we sat in our cockpits on standby, taking off when a red flare was fired from the duty hut. The field was wide and covered with white chalky dust and bomb splinters, and when we refuelled after a scramble we just stayed in the aircraft. The bomb craters that regularly pocked the landing area were usually quickly filled by ground personnel, but attrition was high and the pilot casualty rate was so serious that one never got to know everyone in his own squadron. I had been promoted to Flying Officer at the beginning of the month, but rank at Malta had nothing to do with one's designation in the air. We had to start all over again as wingmen to those who already had experience in the different type of tactics which were used out there, and it was not unusual to see Flight Lieutenants, Squadron Leaders and even Wing Commanders who were just out from the UK, flying No2 to veteran Sergeant Pilots.

In a skirmish over St Paul's Bay the day after reporting to 229, my machine was hit by fire from an Italian Reggiane fighter and I nearly fell victim to the stories we had heard in England that the Italians were not really competent at air combat. This analysis was not necessarily true at Malta and some of the Macchi pilots especially were experienced and dangerous adversaries. The Germans, though, had most of the élite fighter pilots based in Sicily and thus was the enemy force that essentially took the highest toll on the island defenders. The yellow-nose Messerschmitts had to be shown considerable respect and, if one was not constantly alert, he could easily become the prey of these cunning foes. The enemy bombers with the most lethal abilities in the siege were the Ju88s, which were generally utilized as dive-bombers against the airfields and the harbor area. The Junkers had one consistent trait to which they seemed forever faithful in that if they were intercepted before they arrived above the island, they would jettison their bombs and turn back, but if once they had started the run onto their selected target nothing but a direct hit would stop them.

It was mostly sunny at Malta, and sometimes there was haze that seemed to exaggerate the murderous rays of the Mediterranean sun. One never became accustomed to the strain and the hunger out there and the only valid reason for not reporting for duty was going down with a case of sandfly fever. With it all, some of the most spectacular air battles of the war were fought above the devastated island. Because of the bombing hazard the Squadron pilots were quartered several miles from the Takali base on a hill overlooking the terrain that led to the sea beyond the airfield. We lived in one of the old two-story dwellings of stone construction that were standard on Malta, and the upper rear section of the edifice possessed a lengthy porch-like balcony which had a view of the sloping terraced fields below. When we were off duty we would sit out there in wicker chairs and watch the parachutes descending. Sometimes the Ju88s would peel off far above and we always thought they were coming straight at us.

I had arrived at Malta during a relatively quiet period and quickly became frustrated with the lack of activity, so one evening I decided to carry out a lone, unauthorized sweep over Sicily. The night was very bright with a full moon. The sortie was, however, diverted about 20 minutes after becoming airborne by a direct order over the R/T from Fighter Control to return immediately to Luqa – the only base then with adequate night operations facility. Upon landing at Luqa, I was greeted after I had alighted from the cockpit by Wg Cdr Grant [the Wing Commander Flying], and informed that I was, to phrase it kindly, confined to quarters. I was returned to Takali the following morning, under escort, and was further informed that I was grounded and confined to quarters until told otherwise. Everyone at Takali, with the exception of the interrogators, regarded the incident as funny, and such was the state of mind and atmosphere at Malta in those days, no one (except the Inquiry Board) ever asked why I did it.

I soon discovered that I was charged with conducting an unauthorized sortie (at night in a day fighter), unnecessary expenditure of ammunition – I had tested the guns over the sea because we had been having instances of cannon jamming – and unauthorized consumption of petrol. There were several other related charges, but the final upshot of the whole thing was that about three weeks later I received summary disciplinary action through HQ Med in the form of a transfer to the Middle East. So, by October, I was packed off to Egypt, flying out in a Dakota. Everyone on board was apprehensive about German long-range night fighters which were known to venture out from Crete and patrol the very air lanes which we were travelling. We landed at Cairo before dawn the next morning. Even with its intolerable swarms of flies, Cairo took on almost the aspect of paradise after Malta, most noticeably in the realm of abundant food and exotic places and activities. I soon learned, however, that the natives were universally despised by the British and Empire forces and this dislike was, in turn, reciprocated at every opportunity by the Egyptians.

All this became academic after I reported to the Almaza transit camp out beyond Heliopolis. For some curious reason – considering the wretched living and operating conditions at Malta – a transfer to a Western Desert unit was considered as being sent to a 'punishment' squadron! As it turned out, the 'punishment' squadron I was posted to was the prestigious and high scoring 92 (East India) Squadron of the Desert Air Force's 244 Spitfire Wing. However, when I arrived at the landing ground, the terrain rivalled that of a moonscape in its desolation and made even Malta appear attractive in retrospect.

Two days later the British offensive known as Second Alamein or, more popularly, the Battle of El Alamein, began. There was no time to be concerned about the flies and the heat. We lived in tents and I had hardly been introduced to the other pilots when, flying the same type of tropical Spitfire V as we had in Malta, I went on the first sortie [on 9 November 1942, flying EP657]. The ground fighting had proved to be predictably fierce and the Spitfires, which were ordinarily reserved for escorting the Kittyhawk and Hurricane fighter-bombers, were ordered onto strafing operations but were pulled off the duty within the week because of losses and heavy damage to the aircraft. On one of these low level missions near Sidi Barrani we were attacked from above by some Messerschmitts of JG27 and lost two of the Spitfires. As we returned to base on the deck there were burning hulks of armored vehicles and lorries nearly as far as one could see across the arid landscape. That same week Montgomery's Eighth Army broke completely through the enemy resistance and the long Axis retreat out of Egypt and across Cyrenaica and Tripolitania had begun. Many cold nights in the desert lay ahead.

As the Afrika Korps and what was left of the Italian forces withdrew, the Desert Air Force moved forward behind the army units. We usually occupied the former Luftwaffe landing grounds after they were technically cleared of mines. On the airfields immediately beyond Alamein there were hundreds of abandoned enemy aircraft in every form of dismal disarray. The strains of 'Lili Marlene' began to fade and die.

By mid-November 1942 we were nearing Tobruk and the Squadron was joined by another pilot who was to become a distinguished British ace, Flg Off Neville Duke. At the time that he arrived at 92 Squadron, which incidentally was a Battle of Britain unit and one of the highest scoring in the RAF, Duke had already completed one operational tour in the Middle East and had downed eight enemy aircraft. At the end of the campaign he would have raised that figure to 19 and would add even more in the Italian operations of the following year. I had the opportunity that autumn and winter to fly in company with him. As with George Beurling, I was forever impressed with the natural qualities he exhibited in air fighting; the keen instincts, the exceptional eyesight, the total co-ordination, qualities which as a whole were denied the average fighter pilot of that era. A middle-class Englishman, 21-year-old Duke was quiet and deceptively unassuming and at times displayed a sense of humor toward the absurd, as if laughing at the monumental farce in which fate had cast us.

In January 1943 the new year found us at Misurata in Tripolitania and during this period we were plagued by Messerschmitt fighter-bombers. They would come in low and fast and sometimes they would catch us without warning; when we did scramble in time we had to be quite cautious because they were always escorted by a high cover. We lost one pilot over the airfield because of this arrangement. When February arrived, 92 was stationed at Castel Benito and I had nearly completed my first operational tour. We were conducting escort missions to the Mareth Line in southern Tunisia and on one of these sorties I was attacked by a Messerschmitt, which admittedly I did not see, and hit in the head by a shell fragment. In a way the incident is somewhat strange in its own context. I was with four other 92 Squadron Spitfires and a couple from 601 Squadron on patrol south-west of the Mareth Line. We began to get a considerable amount of ground fire at about the same time someone reported 109s going into the sun at eleven o'clock. I had no sooner looked in this direction when I was struck in the right side of the head with what was later proved to be either 15mm or 20mm shrapnel. I didn't see anything and had no idea where it came from except that it sliced parallel from the top of my ear to my left eyebrow, slitting my helmet somewhat and cutting my goggle straps. I began to bleed profusely from that side and instinctively took evasive action in a sharp downward turn to port. The strange part was that I saw no other aircraft at the time, not even Spitfires let alone 109s. The other strange factor was that there seemed to be no other damage to the aircraft, as indeed was the fact as I found out later. At any rate I proceeded to our advanced base west of Tripoli where I landed and was greeted with a certain amount of curiosity and apprehension by the groundcrews. After being conveyed to a field hospital where a couple of pieces of shrapnel were still in the wound, I was transferred to a rear base hospital in Cairo where I remained for two weeks. By that time the wound was considered to be healing and there were no more shrapnel splinters to be removed although I was cautioned by one doctor that I had possibly received nerve-ending damage to some of the trauma leading to my right eye.

At Cairo in March I was finally discharged from the military hospital and was scheduled for an instructor's assignment at an OTU near Port Said. At the time I was approached by an American Colonel who was a

---

Leo was involved in two successful combats during January 1943. On the 7th, in a fierce dogfight with Bf109Gs of II/JG77 which cost 92 Squadron two Spitfires, he claimed one Messerschmitt probably destroyed while flying ER473. The following day, when flying EP788, he engaged a number of Bf109Gs ten miles west of Tamet and after a tough dogfight eventually shot one down into the sea.

liaison officer with General Brereton's US 9th Air Force Headquarters and induced to transfer to the USAAF. I was, to a certain extent, reluctant to leave British service because by that stage I had become immersed in the RAF tradition and the American procedures seemed quite foreign. However, a deadline had been set by the US authorities for RAF transfers that spring and, on the last day of March, I was released from the RAFVR and inducted into the Army of the United States (Air Corps) with the rank of Captain.

The 9th Air Force in the Middle East at the moment contained only one Fighter Group, the 57th (Black Scorpions) which was equipped with P-40 Warhawks and had served at the front since July 1942. We had escorted them at intervals when I was with 92 Squadron and they were later to figure prominently in what became known as the 'Palm Sunday Massacre' off Cap Bon in April 1943. I was initially assigned to this Group but before I reported back to Tunisia the orders were changed and I was returned to the US in the role of combat instructor. So ended my two years with the Royal Air Force and as I boarded the transport flight and said goodbye to the sights and smells of Cairo, many reminiscences occupied my thoughts. Though the British did not actually record missions by the number, I had participated in about 110 operational sorties since that first day with the Eagles at North Weald. Curiously, circumstances were to dictate that I would never return to operations for the remainder of World War II.

As it is with all who return from a journey, I was happy to arrive home again, but with the war had come changes and it was not outwardly the same country that I had departed in the summer of 1941. The conflict, of course, was not at the nation's doorstep as it was in Europe and Asia but the aura of war was everywhere and the military forces were esteemed by civilians to such a degree that as a former RAF combat pilot I suddenly found myself to be, however briefly, a celebrated curiosity.

The time I spent with the USAAF during the rest of the war was really an anti-climax after all the actions of the early years, but combat instruction on fighters in those days was not without its excitement and tragedy. I also met many of the American pilots who would play a vital part in the air war over Europe in the final phase. Assigned to the 81st Fighter Squadron of the 50th Fighter Group (cadre OTU) at Orlando, Florida, I settled rather awkwardly into the the new routine but I soon became accustomed to the much larger fighters (P-47 Thunderbolts) with which the Squadron was issued. In time I learned to like them, though they did not have the same qualities which attracted me to the Spitfire. The pilot training programme in the US had grown to mammoth proportions by 1943 and personnel turnover in the OTU courses was seemingly endless. An average loss of one pilot a week was considered normal and most of these training fatalities were usually related to midair collisions or while performing aerobatics at low altitude. The part played by instructors in these cadre units was both nerve-wracking and dangerous because of the high amount of hours flown daily on all sorts of missions in conjunction with accompanying inexperienced pilots. But my only serious confrontation with disaster in this category came as the result of colliding with a tree-top during ground-target gunnery practice. The Thunderbolts were so sturdy that I landed without any problem with a large portion of the tree embedded in the leading edge of the port wing.

I was joined at this unit, whose specific purpose it was to ready pilots for operations in the European Theater, by other fighter veterans including a few from the former China Volunteer Group, the Flying Tigers. When, in March 1944, the 81st itself was ordered to England (later to be involved in air cover for the D-Day landings), I was transferred to the 438th Fighter Squadron at Fort Myers, an organization that also flew P-47s and had a similar OTU programme, but I was then hospitalized for several months following an accident. Upon convalescing I was assigned to another Thunderbolt fighter unit (53rd Fighter Group) and was due for embarking back to the UK, but by then the war was dissipating to its termination in Europe. I did not wish to remain with the peacetime service, so I returned to civilian life. After the roar of the past five years there seemed to a deafening silence.

The immediate postwar years were, for many who had served, a period of sometimes difficult adjustment to civilian life. If not disillusionment, then certainly frustration became a daily experience. I stayed in the aviation field because I had no other trade, and after a time as a demonstrator for a light aircraft company in California, I supplemented my subsistence with employment as a crop-duster and by performing aerobatics at small town air shows with a pre-war Stearman biplane. I was pursuing this uncertain profession when, in the spring of 1948, the Palestine issue and the formation of the Jewish State of Israel came into world-wide focus. It seemed clear that after what had happened to the Jews in Europe during the war and by the fact that they were, in Palestine, surrounded by hostile Arab nations who had vowed their annihilation, that here was not only a political and military crisis but a moral issue that one could not, in conscience, ignore. It also became obvious after 14 May 1948 [the official date of the ending of the British Mandate in Palestine] that the Jews were in desperate straits in their lack of military aircraft and of qualified personnel with operational abilities. By the end of the first week of the escalating conflict I had offered my services by letter through the Jewish Agency in New York and on 30 May 1948 I was accepted as a [non-Jewish] foreign volunteer in the Israel Defense Forces.

PREAMBLE

When the Jewish national homeland of Israel became a reality in mid-May of 1948, the problems which had accumulated for the new State were manifold and formidable. Defense of the partitioned Palestine boundaries against attacks by Arab bloc countries, whose alliance advocated destruction of the Jews, was the immediate and primary concern – and containment of the invaders in the initial stage was due in large measure to the resourcefulness and individual courage of the meagre Israeli forces. The serious lack of advanced war material and of arms in general caused the situation to be critical during the first weeks, and determination became a virtue that was almost mandatory within the defense units. An absence of co-ordination among the Arab armies afforded some respite but the position of the emerging nation remained precarious as the month progressed. Although the UN had assigned a mediator and a force of peace-keeping observers to the Middle East in an attempt to settle the dispute and end the fighting, it was recognized that the ultimate security for the Jews lay in military strength.

In addition to external pressures, the new government was plagued from within by increasing dissension between Haganah* and the extremist Irgun Zvai Leumi* (IZL) faction. David Ben-Gurion's moderate Haganah, supported by the internationally active Jewish Agency for Palestine, was firmly established as the ruling body but there was an ever-widening ideological gap between the two political elements and there was no hint of reconciliation on the horizon. As the month of May continued, the problems demanded a rapid solution because it was not only victory or defeat at stake, but the survival of the Jewish nation itself. One of the pre-requisites to this survival was to build an air force.

---

* Haganah was the military arm of the Jewish Agency; Irgun Zvai Leumi (National Military Organization) was classified as a terrorist organization by the British, as was the breakaway Lohamei Heruth Israel (Fighters of Freedom of Israel), better known to the British as the infamous Stern Gang, named after its notorious founder Avraham Stern, killed in a police raid in 1942.

When April ended that spring and the termination of the British Mandate loomed, Haganah was faced with preparing for the defense of the Yishuv (the Jewish population in Palestine) against the impending threat of Arab air attacks. With no suitable warplanes available, the multitude of complexities inherent in organizing an air force from nothing became obvious and dismaying. The Jewish leaders knew that concerted efforts must be made to procure combat aircraft and experienced personnel from abroad. The foreign volunteers who responded during these crucial months were to become part of what can only be described as a gallant band.

At a time when the Allies of World War II were scrapping guns and planes, the British blockade of arms to Palestine prior to May 1948 made the delivery of any aircraft almost impossible. Although the American [and British] public was generally sympathetic to the Jewish cause, the United States government was strict in its enforcement of the embargo which forbade arms exports to belligerents and, mainly as a result of British pressure, most European countries followed suit.

Parked on airfields in the United States were thousands of war surplus aircraft which were being sold at a fraction of cost. A limited number of transport planes (C-46 Commandos) among these were secretly purchased by Haganah and flown out during May under Panamanian registry. The air cargo carriers which were an element of this episode were to prove providential in the months to come and were, in fact, to be the nucleus of the Israeli Transport Command.

The arms embargo by the Western powers, however, which they had foreseen, had prompted the realistic Israelis to search elsewhere for the vitally needed arms and machines. These provisions were to come from the newly formed Communist state of Czechoslovakia. A month before the Declaration, an underground purchasing mission had negotiated for some Messerschmitt fighters which the Czech factory at Prag-Cakovice had manufactured for the Germans during World War II. After the hostilities started in Israel, the question of how to get these machines to their destination was resolved by the decision to dismantle them and transport them inside the cargo carriers, thus at once solving the matter of secrecy and the dilemma of how otherwise to fly short-range fighters across thousands of miles of unfriendly European territory.

The first Messerschmitt to be sent to Israel in this manner was transported by a chartered American Skymaster (C-54) on the airlift route which became known as Operation Balak. In conjunction with the arrival of the initial fighters, the first group of foreign volunteer and Palestinian Jewish pilots, who had been hurriedly trained on the difficult-handling Messerschmitts at Budejovice, were returned to Israel. Czech technicians accompanied the early aircraft deliveries to supervise their re-assembly at the Israeli airbase at Aqir. The C-46s from the deal in the US, which were then arriving in Europe, were immediately put into service on the Balak run and, by the end of May, four of the Messerschmitts were operational. Israel's first fighter squadron was born.

From 15 May to 29 May, the date that the Messerschmitts went into action, Jewish airspace had been completely controlled by the Arab air forces. While it was true that the Syrians and Iraqis in the north and central sectors were rather primitive as far as air power was concerned, the Royal Egyptian Air Force operating from the south possessed some of the requirements for a modern air war. Trained and partly supplied by the RAF, the Egyptians had, on the eve of the invasion of Israel, two fighter squadrons composed of 40 Spitfires and two Dakota (C-47) squadrons. Some of the Spitfires had been converted to fighter-bombers and most of the Dakotas were designated for bombing duty as well. The Egyptian base at El Arish in the Sinai became the operational headquarters for the air attacks on the Jewish State.

At the beginning of the conflict on 15 May, the Israelis had, in opposition to the Egyptian force, three flights of light aircraft which were known as the Palestine Flying Club. The majority of these planes were ex-RAF Auster liaison machines and though they were useful in carrying supplies and supporting the isolated settlements, in any type of sustained action they were at the mercy of the Egyptian pilots.

The arrival of more foreign volunteer pilots and the presence of the Messerschmitts were factors that were soon to change the scenario. On 3 June 1948 the Israelis won the first of the aerial victories which in time would produce a measure of air superiority never to be seriously threatened.

* * * * *

This book is a personal account of the author's experiences in Israel's War of Independence, based upon notes maintained at the time, and is essentially a story of the founding of an Air Force and of those who served in it during the first desperate year.

Leo Nomis

CHAPTER I

THE VOLUNTEERS

The noontime sun glares from the pale architecture and dances on the blue surface of the Mediterranean beyond the sea wall. The air is warm and smells of the sea. The city has a holiday atmosphere. Crowds fill the cafes along the beach road and there is the sound of laughter. There are old men in white shirts. They walk slowly and look at women in faded dresses bargaining with shopkeepers in the shade of doorways. But mostly there are soldiers in desert khaki. Sometimes the soldiers are walking arm-in-arm with girls who are also soldiers and always there is laughter. The rifles slung casually, the holstered pistols, the military vehicles on the streets taking nothing from the carnival mood. Colored streamers snap briskly in the breeze above a pavilion near the beach and bathers lie on the ground. It is Tel Aviv in the summer of 1948 and everyone knows that the war is not far away.

I sit at the sidewalk cafe with Bieberman. We drink Palestinian cognac and watch the sunlit street that passes in front of the Gallim Yam. We are volunteers. At the tables about us there are many people and most of them are volunteers too. Music comes from a gramophone inside the cafe. We listen to the music. We have just arrived in the city. It has been two weeks since the day at the Jewish Agency in New York. Now the sea at Tel Aviv sparkles before us. Time and distance have merged the days together – the journey to Rome and Haifa and the ride to Petah Tiqva with the others...

* * * * *

It was humid in New York and at the Jewish Agency office on 58th Street there was a crowd and we had to wait around for a while. I meet Bieberman. We aren't in the same group but we talk and then we are interviewed by the Agency man with the thick-lens glasses. He gives us some subsistence money and assigns four of us to a room at Claridges. Bieberman had taken a train from Cleveland and I was with the boisterous Schwimmer party from California which had arrived at

Millville, New Jersey, in one of Haganah's surreptitiously purchased Constellations. Everything had been rumor and when we had come up from Philadelphia that morning there was a lot of talk about what was happening in Israel. Everyone still calls it Palestine.

Bieberman is slightly built and he has a thin, well-trimmed moustache which makes him appear dapper. At the hotel he smiles politely and listens to Berger and Goodman. We had ordered drinks in the room and the ice is noisy in the glasses. There are 20 volunteers going through New York in this group and as soon as someone's passport is cleared they are sent out to Rome on the first available airline. The speculations persist about what lies ahead of us. Bieberman is an aircraft engine mechanic. Most of the others are groundcrew also but the curly-haired Berger is a bomber pilot. He and the thin-faced, bespectacled Goodman are talking about the situation. Goodman says that when he volunteered on the West Coast he didn't know whether the Jews even had any airplanes. Berger laughs. He says that Schwimmer has already smuggled some transports out of the States. Goodman looks unimpressed and I think of my meeting wih Al Schwimmer. Smiling and unworried, the heavy-set Schwimmer had ushered me aboard the Constellation at Burbank [California] after the Agency connection in Los Angeles had sent me out there. He had looked at a paper he was holding and, grasping my hand, said he was always happy to see fighter pilots.

The placid-mannered Schwimmer had been a flight engineer with the US Transport Command and after World War II he had formed an aircraft renovating company at Burbank. When, in the spring of 1948, it became obvious that the soon-to-be-declared State of Israel was going to have to obtain aircraft at any cost, Schwimmer approached the Haganah purchasing commission through the Jewish Agency. His proposal, which had initial success, was to buy up surplus transport planes and fly them out to Israel by a multitude of routes after 14 May. The machines subsequently were to be of vital significance in the early operations and most of them served the Israeli military command throughout the war under Panamanian registry. Schwimmer's role of procuring aircraft and crews in the US was to continue into the first months of the summer but it was a precarious role at the time and was soon to have its final performance.

None of us know anything for certain and we are travelling toward the unknown. There is no reason to ask why anyone volunteered. We are all nearly the same age and we are products of World War II and have all endured the disillusionment of its aftermath. It is simple. The Jews are fighting for a homeland in Palestine. They are alone. They can use all the help they can get. Goodman swirls the liquid around in his glass. Berger says he heard that the Jews have German Messerschmitts in Israel. They are getting them from Czechoslovakia. Bieberman looks at me and I look down at the design in the carpet. Two years with the Royal Air Force and another two with the Americans. I look up at the others. We are going to a different war now.

We stay in New York for three days. When Bieberman and I report to the Agency office on the third morning they tell us to be ready to leave that evening. They give us tickets to Rome on BOAC and hand us our passports with Italian visas stamped in them. We don't see Berger or Goodman again. At La Guardia that night we wait to board the overseas flight and we buy a newspaper and read that the UN has managed some kind of ceasefire in Palestine. The evening is warm and we are in shirt sleeves. It is 10 June 1948.

The Jewish Agency for Palestine, originally inaugurated under the British Mandate to mediate Jewish affairs, was the single most efficient body in organizing the immigration of the foreign volunteers to the new State of Israel. With the approach of the summer, expediency in transporting the volunteers to the war was its basic task. Nobody told us what to expect when we got there.

* * * * *

The stars in the dark void over the Atlantic shine brightly and I watch them through the window of the plane. Bieberman sleeps in an aisle seat. Part of the past comes into my thoughts and I remember the other war. The campaigns in Europe and the Mediterranean and North Africa. I look away from the window. I have never been to Palestine before.

We stop over at Bermuda and when we get to Paris the next afternoon we have an hour to collect our bags and change planes for Rome. The airport at Orly is packed with summertime travellers and on the Rome flight the passenger cabin is full. We sit in some rear seats and drink from the bottle of Hennessy we bought at Orly. Bieberman says there is political friction in Israel. The Zionist extremists want a hand in the government but Haganah won't have anything to do with them. Bieberman lights a cigarette. He says that Irgun is too radical. They were underground fighters against the British and a lot of Jews are afraid of them. He says there might be trouble. This observation was to be surprisingly prophetic.

It is night and the city is glittering with lights when we land at Rome. We go through Customs and after we pass the line of uniformed Italians we are met by an Agency man and one of the Haganah contacts. Our passports are returned and we go into the airport lobby. The Israelis are professional and we are told that arrangements have been made for us at the Hotel Roma. The Agency man gives us each 20,000 Lire. Bieberman smiles and the Haganah contact looks at him and says its not worth very much in US currency. They put us in a taxi because they have to stay and meet others and they give us a card with a telephone number on it. The taxi rushes down the boulevards and after we survive the ride into town we feel that we have nothing more to fear from the future.

For some reason we are in Rome for five days and, as in New York, we are told little. They say we will find out in Israel. The postwar influx of tourists and students has converged on the city and the cafes are crowded. We spend most of the time in the cafes or drinking cognac in the hotel room. The second evening, at sunset, the room is filled with soft light and at the table near the window I pour a drink from the bottle and think of why we are in Rome. The incongruities that have taken form in the Palestine war seem almost laughable. The Egyptians with air supremacy! In the Cairo of 1942 the idea of the Egyptians as fighters would have been funny. And the Jews flying Messerschmitts! My mind wanders and other thoughts intrude. 1943. I was shot down by a Messerschmitt 109 over the Mareth Line in Tunisia. I drink the cognac and set the glass in the center of the table. Beyond the window the distant rooftops are all tinted red.

On the fifth morning the Agency man is waiting in the lobby of the Roma. He gives us the usual 20,000 Lire and says that we will be leaving for Haifa tomorrow. The street sounds are loud through the open doors and the Agency man beckons us closer. He says we are not over here for fun. In the afternoon we go to a cafe for lunch. We are finishing the meal when Stein comes in. Stein is one of the mechanics who was with us in New York. He pulls out a vacant chair and sits down. He says he has heard the story on the Messerschmitt deal from one of the volunteer transport pilots. Bieberman orders ice cream. Stein is swarthy and has a bull neck and he says that the Israelis bought 25 Messerschmitt fighters from Czechoslovakia and are delivering about four of them a week to the airfield at Aqir [see Appendix II]. They are transporting them in the C-46s that Schwimmer smuggled out of the States. Stein has more information. He says the arrangements for the Messerschmitts were made two months ago but they couldn't get them down until May. A fighter squadron has already been activated in Israel which consists mostly of foreign volunteers and eight of the Messerschmitts are now in service. Stein says that the commander of the fighter squadron is a Palestinian Jew who shot down two Egyptian bombers over Tel Aviv on 3 June. Stein stands up. He has to go because in the evening he is travelling to Czechoslovakia. He is going to take a course on the modified Junkers engines. He says that the Jewish pilots are trained on Messerschmitts at Budejovice. He wants to know where we are going. We tell him Haifa.

At Urbe airfield on the outskirts of Rome the morning is clear. We take our bags from the taxi and go into a wooden flight shack. Our passage is booked on an unscheduled airline called Pan African which is due out for Athens and Haifa. Inside the shack we meet Meyer Bernstein and an Israeli girl, Sarah. Bernstein is from Chicago and he was a machine-gunner on heavy bombers in World War II. He has been in

Rome for a week but we have not seen him before. Sarah is a Palestinian Jewess who is on a special assignment in Rome and is returning to Israel. Her Haganah service job is with the airborne medical corps and she has been asked to escort us as far as Tel Aviv. Sarah is quiet and plain and she is wearing a military blouse over a light skirt. She sits down in one of the corner chairs. The rest of us go outside and stand in front of the shack in the morning sunlight.

Bernstein is tall and dark and he displays a certain nervousness. He points down to the far end of the airfield. He say that is where Beurling was killed on 20 May. Beurling, a Canadian Gentile, was flying one of the Norseman reconnaissance planes out to Israel and when he took off the aircraft blew up and became a ball of fire, and it crashed into the middle of the runway. Bernstein waves his arms. He says it could have been sabotage. I look over toward the runway. There is still a charred spot there. I look away. I think of Malta that terrible summer [1942] when we never had enough to eat. We were in the RAF then. Beurling was the leading ace out there and he was young and blond and skinny, and everyone called him Screwball.

The flight crew arrives. They are British and they are laughing about something. Without knowing what it is, we laugh too. The aircraft for the trip is a dirt-streaked DC-3 parked down the line. Some mechanics are still working on it.

An hour later we leave Rome behind and climb toward the Adriatic. Bieberman and I sit together and Bernstein and Sarah have the seat in front of us. There are five other passengers but none of them speak to us and all of them are looking out the windows. Bernstein talks for most of the journey. He asks Sarah what she thinks about the ceasefire. She speaks so softly we can't hear her answer. No one thinks the ceasefire will last. Both sides are violating it every day.

Haifa appears off the port wing in the late afternoon. It has the look of all Middle East cities, white in the lowering sun. The transport cuts across the harbor and there are ships at the docks and then we come around to the south and sink onto the chalky surface of the airfield. We are in Israel.

It soon becomes evident that the British are still here. When we arrive at the line in front of the white Customs building there is a British sentry on duty near the entrance. The engines become silent and everyone moves to the rear door. We take the bags from the empty seats and Bernstein asks Sarah what the British are doing here. Sarah smiles and looks at her watch. She says they have authority at the port and the airfield because they are guarding the oil refineries in the north. We get out of the plane and pass by the sentry. He is tanned and his shirt and shorts and beret are dusty. He has flat blue eyes and he glances briefly at us when we go in. His rifle, which has a short bayonet fixed to it, is planted in the dirt at a forward angle and he stands with feet apart. We walk inside and Sarah takes our passports to a long counter where some Israelis are busy checking papers. We look at one another. We seem out of place. Our American slacks are baggy and Bieberman has on a white dress shirt. A khaki-clad Customs man is speaking with Sarah. They speak in Hebrew. We don't know what they are saying because none of us understands Hebrew. Sarah comes over with our passports and says there is transportation outside to take us to a military hostel. We look inside the passports. They are not stamped.

We ride to the hostel in the back of a lorry that swerves through narrow streets and up hills for 20 minutes. The driver is a young Jew in an undershirt. When we get to the hostel we discover that it is an old villa in the eastern section. There are two large wings to it and wide steps lead up to a terrace. There is an untended garden on one side. Sarah stays in the truck and goes around to the womens' compound. Dusk is over the city when we take our bags and go up the steps. The air is warm.

Inside we enter an enormous room that is full of talking people. Most of the occupants are lying on straw pallets on the floor. We put the kit in a corner which is already piled high with personal gear of every description. Everyone in the room is in various stages of undress. Bernstein motions to one who is reclining in only a pair of shorts and asks him what this place is. The one in the shorts leans on his elbow. He says this is a transit camp for foreign volunteers.

We find the mess hall and get a tin plate of lentils and a piece of rye bread and take seats at a wooden table. The mess hall is crowded. We sit across from two South African Jews who have been here for a day. They know more than we do. The room is illuminated by shaded overhead lights and all of the windows are open. The South Africans ask us what we do. We tell them. They smile. They say that they are here to join the Palmach. They are refering to the name given the Haganah front-line defense units. One of them says that there are volunteers here from all over the world. The other one says he saw an Oriental Jew yesterday. Though it is night we have to wave flies away from the food. Bieberman brushes violently at one. Bernstein says that we are from the States. The South Africans smile and say they have already noticed that. We finish the meal and get up. The South Africans continue to smile at us. Their tropical army shirts are wrinkled and show damp streaks down the back. We go out and near the mess hall entrance they are selling seltzer water for five mils. We don't have any Palestine money. Bieberman buys three bottles for a 25 cent piece.

Some of the lights have been turned off by the time we find vacant pallets. We lie down and take off our shoes. Ceiling rafters travel the length of the white-washed walls and I stare up at them for a while. It seems a long time since morning.

We awaken at daybreak. It is not voices that wake us but the flies alighting on our faces and feet. The windows at the far end of the room are open and screenless. Many of those in the room are over on the southern side where there is a wash trough and latrines. The early light shows through the windows and it is already hot. Bernstein is four pallets away but Bieberman has the one next to me. I look at Bieberman. He is sitting up and holding his hands to the side of his head. I get up and make my way to where we left our gear and change into some khakis. I change leaning against the wall. I watch the scene. There are rich and poor, good and bad here. They are all veterans of some war, some army, some oppression. Survivors of concentration camps are here. Nice Jewish boys from affluent families are here. Jews from the ghettos and from every section of any city are here. Christians are here. It doesn't matter who anyone is or who they were – what matters is that they are here. They are volunteers.

We have some tea and bread and then walk out to the terrace. The bright rays of the morning sun flash through the leaves of the trees in the garden. Bernstein joins us and in a few minutes Sarah comes around through the garden. Bernstein asks her what we are supposed to do. Bieberman is still wearing the same clothes as yesterday and Bernstein has on a bright orange polo shirt. Sarah smiles weakly. She says there is a jeep here to take us to Tel Aviv. There is something about her which causes one to feel sorry for her without knowing why.

When we get down to the road with the kit there are lorries parked on the embankment. Some are already loaded with people and they shout back and forth between the vehicles. A jeep is near the head of the line and Sarah motions us in. The driver has a creased, brown face and he is wearing a tattered British Army beret. He speaks English with a heavy Hebrew accent. We all get in and Sarah sits in front and we lunge out in front of the trucks and curve down the hill. We go behind the city and onto a sloping road and we can see the oil storage tanks to the north. The sun has climbed higher and it is warm on our backs as the jeep turns out toward the coast. We come to a stop where the road intersects the Haifa-Tel Aviv highway near Cape Carmel. Off to the right are rows of barracks. The road has been rushing past and I don't see the checkpoint until we halt at the barricade. Bernstein is talking and Sarah turns and motions us to be quiet. Four British soldiers have emerged from an open hut next to the barrier. Three of them have tommy-guns on slings and the other is an officer who has a revolver in a holster. The officer's mouth forms a contemptuous smile which curls downward and the faces of the others are blank. Their appearance is tough and unfriendly and when I see the green berets I whistle under my breath. The British must consider the Haifa area a priority to have the Royal Marine Commandos down here. We are close to the sea and I look across the beach and far out over the blue water. The sky is bright and some gulls are settling on the sand where the tide has made a wide arc. I don't look at the British commandos. It is a different time. Another country.

The officer wants to see the destination papers. The driver looks in a dusty map case on the floor of the jeep and hands a folded chit to the Englishman. The officer, still smiling, looks at it and makes a complete circle of the vehicle. He seems amused with the situation. He returns the paper and turning his back, thumbs us on. One of the soldiers impassively raises the barricade arm and we pass through to the open highway.

On the south road the sea stretches away to one side and inland the brown hills rise beyond the coastal plains. We pass Israeli lorries but the traffic is not heavy and at midday we stop at the beach town of Natanya. We park on a narrow street behind some army trucks and the driver produces a cardboard box containing knishes. One of the Haganah soldiers in the lorry ahead of us yells in Hebrew. The jeep driver makes a gesture and pushes his beret to the back of his head. He gets out and goes into one of the stores across the street. The store has a sign in Hebrew and English. When the driver comes back he has some bottles of seltzer. We eat and drink and we stay in the town for an hour. We can hear the rolling of the surf beyond the beach front. It is hot. Sarah says that the Arab salient is across from us at Tulkarm. The enemy is only ten miles away.

We pull out of Natanya and continue down the coast toward Tel Aviv. Several times we see people in Arab dress tending goats beside the highway. I look over at Bieberman. He shrugs. The terrain becomes flatter and we swing eastward on a dirt road. It is afternoon and on both sides the ground is shaded by a line of trees. We pass a village that has seen fighting. There are heaps of rubble about and, farther along, a burnt-out vehicle. A larger town lies ahead. It is Petah Tiqva. Before reaching the town we turn onto a road that is bordered by an olive grove. Behind the olive grove are some low white-washed buildings. The tyres of the jeep throw out a trail of dust as we turn through an open barbed-wire gate into a large compound. We are waved to a stop by an Israeli sentry in worn British fatigues. We are at the Haganah security barracks at Tel Litvinsky.

The compound is not as crowded as the hostel was and we drive around to an administration hut where we are met by a Haganah official. The Israeli has thin legs revealed by his tropical shorts and he is bald. He indicates that we are to take our kit to the nearby barracks room. The motor of the jeep continues to run and we get out. The driver has one foot propped against the dashboard. Sarah says goodbye. They are going on to Tel Aviv and when she leaves in the fading afternoon light she looks back for an instant and then the jeep disappears behind the trees.

The barracks are hot. We are assigned cots and Bieberman sits on the edge of one and stares out at the compound through a window. Half-naked men are lying on some of the cots and others are coming in from an outside shower beyond the rear door of the barracks. We go out and wash.

Before the evening meal we sign papers. We sit at a narrow table in the administration hut and sign the rules and regulations of the Haganah military forces. When we sign them the bald Israeli gathers the papers and takes them over and puts them on a bridge table that is being used as a desk. He looks at us. He has a naturally cynical expression but he also has an indefinable quality which causes him to be likable. He says our passports were not stamped at Haifa so as far as anyone else is concerned we are not here. He smiles wryly. He says that since we are serving with the Haganah forces we are, militarily, Israelis and we will report to Service Headquarters in Tel Aviv tomorrow. He nods and we get up and we all smile automatically and we go out and find the mess hall. After dark we lie on the cots in the barracks and we talk for a while and Bernstein wishes he was back in Chicago.

In the morning the olive trees shimmer in the rising heat of the day and we wait beside the barracks for transportation. Five others are also waiting and everyone is dressed in a different combination of desert khaki. We are the only American volunteers in the group. A lorry stops near the administration hut and we walk over to it. The lorry is an open-back British type with a gun swivel on top of the cab and the windshield is covered with a film of dust. There are four people in the rear section already and we climb up over the tailgate with the others. Bernstein is the last one and he hands the bags to us and then vaults up into the back. The driver has a handkerchief tied around his head. He is wearing sunglasses and he leans from the cab and talks in Hebrew with someone in front of the hut. In a moment the gears grind and we lurch toward the gate and out of the compound.

The distance to Tel Aviv is not far but we stop three times to pick up hitchhikers. When we get to the suburbs the truck is jammed with people and equipment. Soldiers, girls, rifles, knapsacks. I sit next to Bieberman against the side railing. Bernstein is standing at the front near a dark-haired girl whose skirt is too short. He is trying to talk above the rushing wind. No one is wearing any insignia or rank and there is a shortage of headgear. I look at the rifle someone has propped on the railing. It is a German Mauser.

Through the spaces in the side I watch the streets pass. The streets are tree-shaded and the structures are neat and symmetrical. The sun is so bright that the shadows beneath the trees look black. We move through the suburbs and into the congested activity near the beach front. The traffic is heavier here but no one seems to slow down. We turn off into a motor pool area near the sea wall and everyone jumps down and merges with the crowd. We take our kit and jump down also. Across the beach road we can see the water and the salt spray drifts over to us. The driver comes around from the front. He points to a large grey building a half block away. He says that is the Yarkon Hotel. The Yarkon is the Service Headquarters in Tel Aviv.

At the sandbagged main entrance to the Yarkon the sentry can see that we have just arrived. He waves us in. The first floor is crowded and we leave our gear at the doorway and try to find someone who can tell us where to report. The tiled walls are cool but the air is heavy inside and perspiration is beginning to roll down the side of Bieberman's face. There are a lot of volunteers standing around and Bernstein questions some of them. I look at the crowd. Many are wearing side arms and some have the holsters but no guns. The sound of voices is loud. We are directed to the second floor by one of the American volunteers who had arrived yesterday. He wants to know if we have much patience.

The hotel rooms have been converted into offices. Some are double offices and none of them have any identification on the doors. We wait in the white-tiled hallway for two hours. We wait in a line of volunteers and everyone tries to make jokes and no one knows what they are talking about. When we get into the office we are issued a handwritten Hebrew identification card and a book of meal tickets and then we are sent to a second desk for some Palestine currency. The two Israelis at the desks go about the business methodically and a girl with short hair is counting the money. The room is not large and there are too many people packed into it and sounds from outside are coming in through the north windows. We are assigned temporary quarters in Tel Aviv and they tell us to report to the Air Force section in the morning. We get out of the office and into the hall and Bernstein wants to go back and ask more questions. Bieberman and I leave and go out into the summer air and find the Gallim Yam and drink cognac.

The Gallim Yam Cafe was a second home to many of the foreign volunteers that June and it was to become so for us in the days that followed. Across the sea wall on the beach road, it was a block from Headquarters and its bar and tables were always occupied. Some of the outside tables were shaded by red and white umbrellas and when the breeze came in off the water it passed all the way through the open bar. There was music and laughter at the Gallim Yam and sometimes there was sorrow.

We are at the Yarkon early the next day. The hour does nothing to diminish the size of the crowd inside. Bieberman and I are billeted in a small hotel near Allenby Road and we have already had a breakfast of sardines and a glass of tea at the Gallim Yam. Bernstein was sent to a room in a pension house behind Ben Yehuda Street. We have not seen him today. On the third floor at Headquarters there is another line of volunteers at the Air Force screening office. When we go in, an official is at a desk that is piled with papers and he has an accent like Sarah. He tells us to be patient – it will be another day before we can be processed. He says to go see the sights and report in tomorrow. He writes our names down in Hebrew. We go back to the Gallim Yam and find a table near the sidewalk. Bieberman looks at his hands and I watch the blue-green breakers roll in behind the sea wall. At Headquarters we heard that the Egyptians had advanced to Isdud before the ceasefire. Isdud is 25 miles from Tel Aviv.

The noon crowd begins to arrive and we order cognac. The tea we had been drinking during the morning hours remains unfinished in the glasses. Two American volunteers sit down in the extra chairs at the table. A waiter brings our drinks and Bieberman pays for them with one of the Pound notes we were alloted. The American Jews eye Bieberman's stateside clothes. They order beer from the waiter. They are young and dressed in khaki and their teeth appear exceptionally white against the tan of their faces. They receive their beer and they drink and say they have been in Israel since the end of May. They are stationed at the airbase at Lydda, ten miles south-east of Tel Aviv, above the dangerous Latrun Junction. They say the town was taken from the Palestinian Arabs the first week of the war. They say the fighting will start again soon. We tell them that we just got here. The volunteers laugh and talk about the problems they had and say we will have them too. They are with the groundcrew at Lydda and they say the Messerschmitt squadron is farther south at Aqir.

Bieberman goes to the bar and gets two more steins of beer and brings them to the table. The volunteers smile. They begin to tell us stories about the Egyptian fighter-bomber raids. They say two soldiers were killed near the sea wall not far from where we were sitting. They say that the bodies were mangled and were not removed for a while and a lot of flies had gathered. Bieberman looks at me. His mouth is turning upward on one side in a twisted smile. The groundcrewmen say that there haven't been any daylight raids since the two Dakotas were shot down. That was over two weeks ago. They say that Mordecai Alon shot them down and that he is the first air hero of Israel. I look down toward the beach. The war is little more than a month old. One of the volunteers is describing the Dakota incident. He says the Dakotas bombed the central bus station. They simply rolled the bombs out of the side door of the transport plane. Then a Messerschmitt had appeared in the sky. The Dakotas tried to get away but both were shot down. One crash-landed beyond Jaffa and the other caught fire and went into the sea. The volunteer lifts the beer stein. He says that everyone was cheering in the streets.

I was to hear the story in detail in the months to come. How only one of the Messerschmitt fighters had been serviceable at Aqir that morning of 3 June. One Messerschmitt for the air defense of the new State of Israel. The commanding officer of the just activated Israeli fighter squadron took off down the long hot runway of the advanced base some time after the Dakotas were reported coming up the coast from El Arish. The CO is the Palestinian Jew, Mordecai Alon. The Egyptians had appeared unconcerned and methodical. The fact that they were continuing the use of unarmed and unescorted transports as bombers not only displayed an ill-advised contempt for the Israeli defenses, but indicated very uninformed Intelligence sources. The Dakotas reached Tel Aviv and rolled their bombs out and killed some Jews. They were returning home when the Messerschmitt intercepted them.

When the Egyptians became aware of the Israeli fighter's presence they took separate courses toward the south but, climbing above them, the faster Messerschmitt attacked the nearest Dakota and sent it crashing earthward. Mordecai Alon was hampered by the fact that only two machine-guns on the fighter were operating, but it didn't make any difference. The second Dakota crossed the coastline and the Israeli plane closed in behind and fired. A bright flame appeared beneath one of the wings of the Egyptian aircraft. The blaze grew and enveloped the wing and everyone in the streets below could see how bright the flame looked against the blue of the sky. The doomed machine rolled down toward the calm surface of the sea and pieces began to fall from the fiery wreckage. A plume of water and spray and black smoke briefly marked the place where it disappeared. They had met their fate and the drama had unfolded in the cloudless sky above Tel Aviv before ten thousand pairs of eyes. It was a turning point.

In the afternoon we walk back to the Yarkon and we see Sam Lewis coming around the sandbags at the sentry post. Sam Lewis is the pilot who took the Constellation into Millville on the New York run from Burbank the first week of June. He remembers me and smiles. We stand to one side of the Headquarters entrance to avoid the flow of people. Lewis says that the same Constellation is down at Aqir. He is going back to Czechoslovakia in the evening and he is in a hurry to get over to the Park Hotel. He says that Schwimmer was in Miami and that Goodman and Berger are at Zatac.

After Lewis leaves we stand in front of the Yarkon. We are wondering what to do when Bernstein comes out. He says he has his swimming trunks on under his clothes and he wants us to go down to the bathing beach with him. We all walk to the north end of the sea wall where it slopes into a wide stretch of sand. There are others there but it is not really crowded and we sit on the sand. The sand is hot and the tide rushes in farther down. Foam from the waves glides inward and then recedes. The breeze sometimes carries a trail of mist from the tops of the incoming breakers. People splash in the surf. Bernstein takes off his trousers and shirt and begins to sun himself. He received the same news as we did at the Yarkon except that it was embellished by the information that they didn't have a bomber for him to be a machine-gunner in yet. But he is optimistic and cheerful because he has heard a rumor that some B-17s might be smuggled in from the States, and they are considering sending him up to the airfield at Ramat David near Nazareth where they are planning to organize a bomber squadron.

Bieberman and I sit on the sand and watch the bathers. Bernstein goes in the water and when he comes out he starts a conversation with a girl sitting nearby. She comes over and joins us and she can tell that we are volunteers before Bernstein informs her of the fact. The girl is laughing. Her name is Ruth. She is wearing a black bathing suit and she is eighteen years old. She is a sabra. All of the Palestinian Jews are called sabras. Bernstein introduces us. The girl laughs again. She has a nice laugh.

We lie on the soft, flat surface and talk. I can see the jetty at Jaffa curving out into the blue water down the coast. Sunset is near and in a little while Ruth says that she has to go. She wants us to come and meet her parents who have an apartment over beyond Rothschild Boulevard. Bieberman doesn't want to go but Bernstein does, and he and Ruth insist. We all stand up. Ruth ties a skirt around her waist and Bernstein gets dressed and we walk back to the sea wall. Some of the shops and cafes along the beach front are already showing dim lights from the interiors. There is only a partial blackout in effect in Tel Aviv and on Allenby Road a lot of people are on the sidewalks. We pass two cinemas and both are showing Eddie Cantor films. Most of the time we have to run across the streets because of speeding vehicles. We turn up a side road and come to a block of flats with trees in the front yard. Ruth and Bernstein are walking ahead and when we get to the door of the second floor apartment the parents smilingly greet us and gesture us in.

Bieberman looks at the mezuzoth on the door frame as we pass through into the main room. The place is small and has old leather furniture, and there are old vases on the tables. We all seat ourselves at a round lamplighted table in the center of the room. The mother is frail and courteous and the father is courteous too. He has sallow skin and he limps when he walks. They insist that we have some cakes and sweet wine, and while it is served they all talk. The father is a watchmaker and has a shop off Allenby. They had the foresight to get out of Germany in the twenties and Ruth was born in Palestine. So was one of their sons. He is serving with the infantry at Jerusalem. The father pours more wine. He says he was in the British Army with the Jewish Brigade and he was wounded in Italy in 1943. He joined the Haganah Palmach in 1946 but had to give it up the following year because of his leg wound. He says they had too few weapons on account of the British blockade. Bernstein asks him about Irgun. The father and the wife don't change expressions. They shrug. Then the wife says that her family was killed by Hitler. There is a silence for a moment. Ruth gathers the empty plates. She says she is going to join the army next month.

We are back at the hotel. The single room is neat and the two beds are close to the floor. There is a wash basin in one corner. The toilet is outside on the ground floor. From the second-story balcony we can look out on the street below. It is quiet now. Bieberman switches on the lamp between the beds and we talk about what the father said and how all the Jews here are convinced they will win. We have prepared for bed when

Bieberman wants to go down to the Gallim Yam for some ice cream. We go back out.

The street is empty when we walk down toward the beach front. We can hear the surf hissing at the bottom of the road and then we walk into a Stern Gang road block. We are shouted at in Hebrew and we stop walking. In the half light there are two lorries backed up near the end of the street and we don't see them until after we are shouted at. Two soldiers, both short and one wearing a beret, rush up to us. They are carrying Enfield rifles and they both have glowing cigarettes in their mouths. They ram the rifle bolts home and point the barrels in our faces. They persist in Hebrew. They are excited and they act tough and right away we know they are Irgun. Bieberman tries answering in English and then Yiddish. They respond in Hebrew and prod us with the rifles. Bieberman resorts to the ancient gesture of sinking his chin into his chest and raising his palms out. We are nervous and almost laugh. The Stern Gang soldiers don't laugh. They point toward the street entrance behind us and it becomes obvious that they want us to get out of there. We turn around and walk back the way we came. The street is dark and there is silence now but we know that they are there watching us. We turn the corner and the way to the hotel is deserted. When we get to the room Bieberman looks pale and his hands shake and he curses. We are speculating about the incident when a burst of automatic rifle fire echoes down the road outside. A bullet hums above the roof of the hotel. We decide that this is either a normal night in Tel Aviv or that the Arabs may have infiltrated the city.

In the morning the early sun casts an orange glow on the walls opposite the balcony of the hotel room. There is increased gunfire in the streets and toward the beach. We dress and wash and leave the room. We go down the steps to the front of the building. We start out for the Gallim Yam. A soldier with a Sten gun in his hand crosses the road ahead of us, running in a crouch. We begin to run also. We take a narrow street that leads to the beach front and when we reach the first intersection, bullets ricochet from the pavement on the far side. We turn into the rear entrance of the Gallim Yam. More bullets hit out in the roadway and pieces of the surface disintegrate in tiny puffs. There are others already at the cafe and everyone is sitting at the sidewalk tables and looking down toward the bathing beach. Bernstein is there and we join him under one of the red and white umbrellas. We look where everyone else is looking and we can see an LST* lying in the water a hundred yards from shore. Bernstein tells us what happened. It is a clash between Irgun and Haganah and it has gained momentum during the night.

Bernstein points to the ship. The distance from where we are sitting

---

* The LST was the *Altalena*, a former US tank landing ship of the type used during World War II.

is 300 yards but it seems nearer because the air is so clear. The LST is full of arms and Irgun tried to run it up onto the beach and unload it in the darkness of last night. They grounded it on a shoal too far out. Bernstein is incredulous and he says the Jews are fighting each other. The accuracy of his statement cannot be denied. As we watch, a longboat rises on a heavy swell and starts out from the side of the LST. The longboat is white and it contrasts sharply with the dark hull of the larger craft. People and wooden boxes fill the inner space of the longboat and it sits low in the water. The oars begin to pull for the shore. Rifle fire commences from the rooftops down the seafront road and the firecracker sound of a machine-gun comes from the same direction. Simultaneously, automatic weapon fire begins to flash from the Irgun beachhead in the lee of the sea wall. We can see spouts of water rising beside the longboat as it attempts to travel the distance between the LST and the rolling surf. Other flashes wink sporadically along the side of the landing craft. We are all out in the open and exposed to the fire but nobody moves. It is like we are in front row seats at a theater and the play has already begun. We look across at the stage. The Haganah gunners are picking off the men with the oars and the longboat is now drifting aimlessly just beyond the breakers. They are not rowing anymore. As often happens in war, we watch more in fascination than in horror and I am reminded of a line of Spanish poetry – 'Death came and, with a leaden finger, pointed to her victims one by one'.

The confrontation between Irgun and Haganah had been, evidently, inevitable. The continued friction had finally erupted into violence that spread from the beach into the streets of the city. In a move calculated to strengthen their military position and, consequently, their political bargaining position, Irgun had arranged to have a large quantity of arms landed at Tel Aviv. With considerable secrecy the LST operation had been organized at a southern European port and the crew were volunteers. Under the cover of night the vessel, loaded to capacity with weapons, was steered in from the Mediterranean toward the bathing beach. Certain things began to go wrong almost immediately. The craft, which was supposed to be maneuvered directly onto the shore, became stranded on a sand bar a hundred yards out. Other factors intervened. The Irgun vehicles near the seafront, which were to receive the transfer of the arms from the ship, were discovered by Haganah patrols. By then Irgun had passed a point of no return and so decided to fight. Before dawn the Stern Gang had occupied some strategic points around the city. Road blocks and barricades were in turn set up by the Haganah forces and, as the sun rose, it appeared that a Jewish civil conflict, in the midst of a current war of survival, was not going to be avoided. Although the fighting was not really widespread or prolonged, the very existence of the confrontation created tragic overtones and, in the end, the challenge failed. Destiny did not decree it would succeed.

Another burst from the beachhead and some of the bullets sing through one of the umbrellas at the Gallim Yam. Everyone jumps up and runs toward the rear exit. There is a strong smell of gunpowder cordite in the air. A table is overturned in the rush and when we get to the street we keep running. Others are already going down the block. The long shadows cast by the rising sun are stretching out behind them.

The rest of the day is strange. Nothing is normal. The crowds are gone from the streets, the shops are closed. The only vehicles are the lorries taking defense troops to positions. We go around to the Yarkon and the ground floor is full of people and everyone is subdued. We can still hear the firing and then two Mills bombs [hand grenades] explode at the end of the street. The detonations are loud and shrapnel whines shrilly past the doorway. We go down to the latrines. Bernstein stays in the latrine too long. Bieberman and I go upstairs to report. We walk up the stone steps and when we get to the third floor there are people lying down in the corridor. We don't know why they are lying down but we find space near a window and lie down too. The window is open and there is a Haganah defense soldier on the roof of the building across the street. Every time someone tries to pass through the corridor he motions them down. No one knows the reason for this but since the soldier is waving a rifle, no one questions it. We lie with our shoulders against the wall. Bieberman tries to light a cigarette but the match goes out. He is upset over what happened at the beach and about the affair last night when we ran into the Stern people. He says we could have been killed.

Two girls in light tan skirts come up the stairway. They both have fair complexions and one of them wears glasses. They don't lie down. They step over everyone and go to the window above us and begin to shout in Hebrew at the soldier on the roof. Those on the floor exhibit consternation and tell them to shut up. The girls laugh and ignore the ones on the floor. The girl with glasses steps on Bieberman's hand. Bieberman curses and everyone looks at him. The girls continue to shout and finally they make the soldier angry and he raises his rifle and puts a round through the upper pane of the window. Glass flies inwards and showers those in the hallway and the bullet ricochets above our heads for a seemingly interminable length of time. The girls lie down.

It is an hour before we get to the office to report and when we go back downstairs there are many waiting to get out at the main door. The sentries are letting them go two at a time and telling them to stay off the roads. We don't hear any gunfire at the moment but someone says the Stern Gang is over on the next street. Our shirts are wet with perspiration when we get outside. There is a Haganah roadblock on the corner and we turn around and walk down past the Park Hotel. At the far side of the hotel three people have been killed. There is no one else around and the scene seems suddenly eerie. Two of the bodies are on the sidewalk and one is in the middle of the street. They look as though they had fallen while they were running and there is equipment scattered about. The body in the street is lying face down and a ribbon of blood has travelled an irregular course over to the gutter. The blood has turned dark brown in the mid-morning sun. We stand at the curb in silence. A warm gust sends a dust swirl down the empty roadway. The pavement is hot and we turn away and walk on until we find a cafe open on Allenby Road. We go in and drink cognac.

Bieberman is preoccupied and he stares transfixed at the table top in the cafe. He talks again about how we could have been killed. He says he didn't come over here to be killed by a Jew. Bieberman wasn't the only one in Tel Aviv that day who was upset about Jews killing Jews. Everyone felt it. Some were angry, many were fearful and all were gripped by sadness. After the Holocaust and the exodus and the underground fighting, it was Jew against Jew. The future of the national homeland was in the balance and they were fighting each other. Regardless of the ideologies and differences that led to this day, it would remain a day of regrets.

By evening the crowds have returned to the streets but we are kept away from the beach by the barriers and the patrols. A pall of black smoke is drifting over the city. We are standing on a corner a block from the Yarkon and when one of the patrols comes by Bieberman asks them what happened. The two Haganah soldiers hold their rifles carelessly and their shirts are soiled with dirt and sweat. They tell us that a Haganah gunboat has shelled the LST and the landing craft is burning. It was also shelled by a howitzer artillery piece that was dragged onto the beach road. They say the fighting at the beach is over.

Except for a few skirmishes and several armed jeep rampages through the streets by the Stern Gang, when the fighting ended at the seafront it was over. The entire Irgun party was either killed or wounded at the beachhead. The weapons on the LST were destroyed or confiscated and only a hulk remained of the ship. There were casualties among the Haganah forces and an American photographer was one of those killed near the Park Hotel. The episode was not easily forgotten but everyone turned back to the war.

There was never another threat to Haganah. The clash resulted in Irgun being outlawed by the Ben-Gurion government and the Irgun leaders who could be found were arrested. The faction, however, remained in force and they were to play a part in other incidents with their independent actions during this eventful year.

In a few days the beach is serene again and soon the only reminder that fighting has passed that way is the hulk of the LST. It was to remain there, silent and pointing inward at the city, during the long summer and into the autumn and winter of the war. Waves would break along its sides and bathers would sometimes swim out to it. Sometimes one would remember the volunteers who brought it to this place and died.

CHAPTER II

OPERATION BALAK

At the end of the week I receive orders to go out to the airfield at Sde Dov for a flight check. Bieberman gets an assignment to the maintenance section at Lydda the same day. We walk to the hotel room from the Yarkon and Bieberman gets his suitcase. I go with him to the motor pool near the beach. We don't say much and he gets on an army supply lorry that is due to leave for Lydda in five minutes. When he gets into the back of the truck Bieberman reaches down and shakes my hand. There is a bullet hole through the tailgate where he is standing. It is afternoon and the sea breeze is fluttering the collar of his shirt. The lorry starts forward and turns into the street traffic and passes from view behind the Yarkon. In a little while I get a ride to Sde Dov.

The Messerschmitts have moved out of Aqir. They had trouble with the fighters on the paved runways and they are now operating from an auxiliary strip near Natanya. The unit has been designated 101 Squadron and a permanent base is under construction at Herzliya. The accident rate has been high. At Sde Dov it becomes clear that if I am to fly fighters I will have to go to Czechoslovakia for indoctrination on the Messerschmitt. The machines have a bad reputation because of certain handling characteristics and the Messerschmitts in Israel are restricted to operational sorties. They are having problems keeping enough of them serviceable. The ceasefire isn't expected to last much longer.

Mischa Keren leans back in the camp chair behind the desk in the operations shack at Sde Dov. He's the CO of the light plane base. He is slim and wears a British bush jacket with no insignia. Articulate and relaxed, he is formerly of the RAF and the Palestine Flying Club. He lights a pipe and sits forward. A paper is on the desk between and he writes across the bottom of it. I look out through the wooden-framed doorway at the field beyond. Sde Dov is on the northern fringe of Tel Aviv near the mouth of the low-ebbed Yarkon River, and the base is so close to the beach that the main strip leads into the sand. There are some trees on the northern border and the patches of short grass on the landing area are burnt brown by the summer sun. During the Mandate there was sport flying here. Now a collection of training craft and the fabric-covered Rapide transports are parked about the perimeter and near the hangar at the eastern end.

The air is clear except for some sea haze to the west and we taxi the Fairchild into the wind and stop near the field huts. The propeller continues its revolutions for a moment after the switches are cut and then it snaps to a halt in a diagonal position. Keren is still laughing about the landing. We had flown in the vicinity of the base for 20 minutes. Keren could see that I was able to fly the machine so he didn't bother to prolong the flight and when we came back in, the landing was too fast and we floated down to the sand. I had to go around and try it again. At the hut line we climb out of the cabin section of the aircraft and stand beside the brownish-colored fuselage. The Fairchild was not an unfamiliar type to me but it is prewar and it is a long time since I operated one. Keren taps the wing strut and laughs. He says it was captured from the Egyptians two months ago. They were smuggling hashish in it when it developed engine trouble on a night flight from Lebanon and was forced to land in the Negev. The Egyptian pilot was interned when the aircraft was confiscated by the Israelis. The Fairchild was initially put into Jewish service with the 3rd Palmach Galil Flight but was later transferred to Sde Dov. It has the blue Star of David on its side.

We walk back to the Operations hut and we hear the sound of a fighter turning high overhead. It is a Messerschmitt and its silhouette is sharply defined against the azure background of the upper atmosphere. Keren squints into the sun and smiles. He says it's still odd to think of the German machines as friendly. He takes his pipe from a pocket and nods toward the disappearing fighter. He says that some of the Egyptian prisoners of war call the Messerschmitts Desert Hawks. We are at the hut and Keren points to a British Auster down the field. They flew bombing raids in the tiny planes during the first days.

The original group of pilots at Sde Dov were already legendary. The base was a prime target for the Egyptian fighter-bombers in the early weeks and the field was shot up with persistent regularity. There was little anti-aircraft defense and the crews would lay on the ground with rifles and fire at the Spitfires, and when the Egyptian planes had gone the Israeli pilots would get in the Austers and take off on missions against the enemy concentrations. The Israeli raids with the light aircraft were ineffective and foolhardy but there was never any hesitation in launching them.

Keren looks toward the low fence on the southern edge of the field. Behind the barbed-wire enclosure of the maintenance area one can see the fuselage of a Spitfire, the green and white crescent and stars of the Royal Egyptian Air Force showing clearly on the dull camouflage of the body. He turns and looks at the Auster again. He talks about one of the missions in May. There were small home-made bombs on improvised racks under each wing of the sport plane. A report had been received that Egyptian motorized units were maneuvering north of Majdal along the coast and the Israeli pilot of the standby Auster took off and headed south, flying low past Tel Aviv and Jaffa. When he reached the enemy area, which was only 15 flying minutes away from Sde Dov, the Israeli pilot saw the vehicles and he circled at 3,000 feet and released the bombs. Bursts from the defensive ground fire began appearing close to the small craft and when the bombs fell they only dropped from one wing. The pilot had to reverse the controls in order to remain upright, The Israeli couldn't see where the departed bombs had hit and while he was struggling with the jammed lever he was attacked by a Spitfire. The Egyptian plane came in so fast it overshot the Auster and, while the Spitfire was turning, the Israeli shook the stubbon bombs loose and dove for home. He frustrated the Egyptian with evasive tactics and when he got over Jaffa the Spitfire broke off the pursuit. The Israeli landed at the Sde Dov base and when he alighted from the aircraft they told him to get ready for another mission to the same target. Keren laughs. In a war of unsung heroes the men of Sde Dov would remain high on the roll of honor.

At the Operations shack two pilots were looking at a wall map. Keren goes around them and at the desk he writes again on a paper in Hebrew. He hands me the paper. He says that he is recommending that I go on up to the fighters but then he looks at me and shakes his head. He says that I will be told at the Yarkon that I have to go to Czechoslovakia to check out on the Messerschmitts. We shake hands and he wishes me luck.

When I return to Headquarters that day I am sent in to see Boris Senior, the sophisticated South African Jew who has a reputation for charm and organizational ability as well as being an experienced pilot. Boris Senior has taken Israeli citizenship and he is to play an important part in Air Force affairs this first year. In the office he stands beside a table and reads the note I brought from Sde Dov. He politely gives it back and, walking to the door, he points out another office farther down the hallway. He says to see Aharon Remez.

Aharon Remez is dressed in a plain khaki shirt and tropical shorts. There is no protocol when I go into the room. He waves an arm at a chair and I sit down. He is to be the first Commander of the Israeli Air Force. He is an inscrutable Palestinian Jew who conducts business with a stern approach that discourages familiarity. Having been a fighter pilot in the RAF, he is only a few years older than I but gives no sign that we have anything in common. He sits at the desk and looks at the wall for a moment and then glances at the paper. He says the CO at Sde Dov has recommended that I go to 101 Squadron but that I will have to go to Budejovice first. Remez gets up and goes to the window and looks at the street. He says the Messerschmitts are bastards and if I am not properly checked out I could be killed quite easily. I will go out on the Balak run from Aqir tomorrow. When he turns away from the window he picks up a telephone and speaks in Hebrew. He hangs up the receiver. He smiles but the smile lacks congeniality.

I stand up. As I start to leave, the CO of 101 Squadron comes in and Remez motions me to stay. Israel's first air hero has fair hair and a strong jaw and blue eyes and he could pass as a German fighter pilot. One of the Messerschmitt pilots is with him. Remez introduces them. Mordecai Alon and Ezer Weizman. Tall, rail thin with classic Hebrew features, Weizman has a debonaire quality which is absent from the personalities of both Remez and Alon. The CO of 101 Squadron looks at me. His face shows nothing. He is reserved, cool. He is undoubtedly a dedicated man. He says he will be happy to have me in the Squadron when I return from Budejovice. He is sorry that I can't be checked out at Natanya but they can't risk the machines. The ominous implications of this statement seem to be considered normal by everyone else in the room. Weizman is sitting in one of the chairs and watching the rest of us with an amused smile. No one talks about operations but Alon asks me what I know about the Messerschmitt. I look toward the window. I think of 1942 and the captured Messerschmitt 109s at El Daba and how we used to sit in the cockpits and manipulate the controls. I remember the cockpits always had a peculiar odor. Alon smiles thinly. He says I will have to know more than that.

* * * * *

The rays of the setting sun slant through from the balcony archway and create a bright patch on the floor of the hotel room. I pack a worn travel bag. It seems strange without Bieberman. We had only been together for three weeks but it seemed longer because of everything that happened. I sit on the edge of the bed. There is a copy of the *Palestine Post* on the other bed and I pick it up – 'Arab Legion Violates Truce in Jerusalem' – 'Bernadotte Leaving Damascus Today' – 'New Stamps Due' – 'Truman on Campaign Tour' – 'Louis Retains Title' – 'The Ordeal of the Negev Settlements' – 'Road Junction Sniping' – I put the paper down. It is yesterday's. I stare at the floor and think about the recent days. They have a different kind of patriotism here. It is not emotional on the surface. It is a determination. It is the all-encompassing confidence and determination that is impressive. It is the mass energy and intellect of a people applied toward a single goal. I go out and stand on the balcony and look down to the crossroad. A pushcart vendor is arguing with someone who is inside the cab of an army truck. The truck is up on the sidewalk. I turn back into the room and finish packing the bag.

I see Bernstein at the Gallim Yam the next day. I left my kit at the Yarkon and was informed that I leave for Aqir in the evening. There was talk at Headquarters about a hospital plane that went down somewhere.

At the Gallim Yam I sit down at the table where Bernstein is having tea. He is due to go up to Ramat David tomorrow and he still talks about the B-17 rumor. He has also heard the story of the missing hospital plane. A Rapide light transport carrying some wounded from a field near Jerusalem failed to arrive at Sde Dov. There were five aboard including a girl and it is assumed that the aircraft made an emergency landing along the coastal flats somewhere north-west of Isdud. There is an air and ground search under way. The tower at Aqir last heard from the Rapide at dawn and then the radio transmissions from the aircraft had ceased. Bernstein pushes his chair back from the table. He says the area where they think the Rapide went down is reputed to be pretty desolate and it isn't occupied by either side. Bernstein says that the pilot of the hospital plane is an American Gentile.

It is almost midnight when the jeep gets to the transport operations building at Aqir. Two of the C-46s are parked near the adjoining hangar and the only light is coming from the interior of the Flight hut. There are three others in the jeep who are crewmen returning from leave in Tel Aviv. It was late when we leave the Yarkon motor pool and we ride in silence on the dark roads. I am the only one getting out at Ops and I take the bag and walk to the doorway. The stucco on one side of the hut is pock-marked from bomb fragments. The air is cooler now. Inside, the Flight hut is busy and it is noisy. Flying equipment is scattered about on the chairs and tables. A blackboard on the far wall has names and numbers written on it. Some Americans, who fly the chartered C-54 for Northern Air Lines out of Czechoslovakia, are lounging on a fabric-covered couch in a corner. Two of the C-46 pilots come over to where I am standing. They know who I am. They are both American Jews and their short-sleeved shirts have grease on them. They say the aircraft isn't ready yet. I put the bag near a wall of the hut and lie down against it.

It is three hours before the co-pilot comes by and says that they are preparing to leave. We go through the field door and the cargo carrier is directly outside. Off to one side in the darkness are piles of crates that were unloaded from the C-54. Most of them are Mauser ammunition boxes. When we get to the loading door of the C-46 we are joined by the pilot and navigator. An intellectual-looking German Jew, the navigator has a small monkey on his shoulder. The monkey jumps up to the top of the navigator's head. The others laugh. There are no other passengers and I wait by the belly steps while they inspect the aircraft. Even in the dim light the Panamanian flag is conspicuous on the tail fin. Operation Balak. The C-46s are the workhorses of the Balak run which brings in the war material from Czechoslovakia. I look up at the wide fuselage and remember the unpopularity of the machines. They were unstable and generally unreliable but in this war they are the backbone of the Transport Command.

One of the groundcrew comes by. He is a foreign volunteer who was with us the first day at the Yarkon and he stops and comes over to where I am waiting for the others. I tell him that I am going to Zatec. The mechanic rests a foot on the extended steps of the cargo compartment. He says they found the hospital plane. They saw it from the air in the afternoon and then a Palmach patrol finally reached it after dark. One of the engines had failed and the Rapide had made a landing on the flats. The plane was intact but everyone on it was dead. Saudi Arabian irregulars had found them. Saudi Arabian irregulars. It was one of the common names applied to the independent guerilla bands who were not under any regular army command, and who had been engaged in actions against the Jews since before the end of the Mandate. The crew of the aircraft and the wounded casualties aboard had been shot and some, particularly the Israeli girl, had been mutilated. The bodies were taken out by the patrol and brought up to Tel Aviv. The pilot was identified as an American. The mechanic is silent after he tells the story and I look past him at the diminishing night beyond the hangar. They were 20 miles from home.

The sky is light with the breaking dawn when Tel Aviv passes behind us and we are on course over the Mediterranean. The cargo space is empty and I sit back against the cabin bulkhead. I can feel the engine vibrations through the panels. In a while the pilot comes back from the cockpit and sits down next to me. He has alert dark eyes and a scar runs jaggedly through one of his eyebrows. He spreads a map on the floor beside us and points to the course. The Balak run is oddly roundabout. Our first stop is at Ajaccio, Corsica. The pilot laughs. He says it's the only place the Jews could make arrangements for refuelling on the route. The French think we are from Tangiers. The pilot's finger traces a line on the map which leads north-east out of Ajaccio and across Italy, passing east of the Alps and then upward until it reaches Zatec in Czechoslovakia. The pilot brushes back his hair. He says he brought one of the C-46s over from the States in May and they had a lot of trouble. The United States Government is depending on the UN to settle the Palestine issue and they are putting pressure on the Jews with the arms embargo. We get up and go into the cockpit section.

There is coffee in a cognac bottle and it tastes bitter but I drink some. The navigator is in the co-pilot's seat and the monkey is perched on the compass above the instrument panel. The monkey studies me with an unblinking stare. The pilot is acting as engineering officer and he sits down in the side seat and lets the co-pilot fly. The engine noise is loud in the cockpit and the pilot raises his voice when he talks. He says they lost their engineering officer on another trip. They were coming into Aqir with a load of guns and ammunition and a dismantled Messerschmitt aboard and when they touched onto the runway the landing gear collapsed. The engineer was taking a nap near the front bulkhead in the cargo compartment and the Messerschmitt fuselage broke loose and crushed him against the plates. No one else was even hurt but it killed the engineer. The pilot lights a cigarette and looks out of the port window. Beyond the wingtip, far to the south, there are broken white clouds close to the sea.

Corsica appears on the horizon and when the craggy mountains of the island become discernible we begin to descend from 10,000 feet. We are on the ground at Ajaccio before noon. The French refuel the C-46 and we go over to the airport cafe for the midday meal. We sit at a wide table in a corner and the food is good and we drink white wine. Fresh air flows through the busy room from the open doorway. Everyone eats and the navigator pours some wine in a glass for the monkey.

When we get back to the aircraft the pilot signs a form that a French mechanic hands him and then, when the engines are started, one of the propellers won't change pitch. The pilot shuts the engines off. He gets out on the wing and lays on top of the nacelle and toys with the propeller mechanism. The co-pilot gets out on the wing also and the navigator and monkey watch from the ground. They try it with the engine running three more times and the third time it works all right, and we all get in. At the front of the runway we wait for a few moments and then the vineyards at the end of the field are falling away beneath us and we are airborne over the sea. It is 1 July.

The airfield at Zatec is 30 miles east of Prague and during the summer of 1948 the Czech base was codenamed Zebra by the Israelis. The weather had begun to deteriorate over Austria and when the runway lights appear there is a steady rain beginning to fall from the darkening sky. We touch down on the wet surface and the lights are yellow through the mist. We turn onto a concrete ramp and swing to a stop near a large hangar. As soon as we drop from the belly steps I see one of the Schwimmer Constellations parked on the apron and, behind a fence beyond the hangar, there are three B-17s. Through the rain, the shapes of the bombers are unmistakeable and I think of Bernstein at Ramat David. The Czech groundcrew and some of the Jews gather around the C-46 and they talk with the flight crew and then we walk over to a wire mesh gate where we are met by two of the Israelis from the Embassy. The crew is going to the Stalingrad Hotel in Zatec and I say goodbye to them and get into a small black sedan with the two Israelis. The Israelis are both silent and they both have on raincoats. I sit in the back seat of the car with my bag and we start out for Prague. The windshield wipers swish monotonously as we go through a guard barrier and on to a slippery two-lane highway. The Czech soldier at the post has a Skoda sub-machine gun slung on his shoulder upside down.

The Israeli arrangement in Czechoslovakia was conducted in an efficient and rather secretive fashion. If the general populace knew anything, there was no outward indication and no one asked questions. The government officials in this most recent of Russian satellites were in control of all the dealing, and the Jews were paying for everything they got. Still, Czechoslovakia, regardless of motive, had to be looked upon as the primary benefactor of Israel, militarily, during this period.

In July 1948 the Israeli Embassy in Prague was comprised of several suites of rooms in a top floor wing of the Flora Hotel. The hotel still had a certain elegance in the old European style but time and wars and austerity had all taken their toll and now, like the Gothic architecture of the city, it was becoming a faded reminder of what used to be. The Flora is near the central railway station and, after almost an hour's drive in the rain, the black sedan stops at the side entrance of the hotel. It is early evening but there is not much vehicle traffic on the streets. Everyone is walking. The taller of the Israelis motions me out and we go through the lobby and up a red-carpeted staircase. Those at the desk pay no attention to us. The Israeli says that I have been assigned an Embassy room for the night.

The room is comfortable but there is something about it that reminds me of the war and I go to the window and watch the rain for a while. I wash and change clothes and the tall Israeli returns and asks for my passport. He leans against the door frame. I give him the passport and he hands me a book of food ration tickets. He never smiles. He says that it won't be necessary to see Ehud Avriel. Ehud Avriel is the Israeli Ambassador to Czechoslovakia. The tall one turns away from the door. He says that I will meet Lichter at dinner. George Lichter is the designated Israeli instructor on the Messerschmitt course at Budejovice. An American Jew with a calm, studious appearance, he had been a fighter pilot with the US 9th Air Force in World War II and he came through Czechoslovakia with the early group. He was held over after the course because a need was discovered for a Jewish liaison pilot at the Czech base. Lichter was considered an excellent pilot but he hadn't been down to Israel yet.

In the dining room off the hotel lobby the driver of the black sedan waves me over to a table adjacent to the entrance. There are two people seated at the table and the driver points to the stocky one and says this is George Lichter. The other is Red Flint. The driver leaves and I sit down and Lichter calls a waiter and orders dinner for me. Flint has exceptionally white skin and he looks too young to have been in the war but he was a US Navy pilot in 1945. At first I don't think he is a Jew but he is. Lichter leans back in his chair and studies me for a moment. He has a short black beard and his eyes are serious. He says that Flint and I will be the last Israeli contingent at Budejovice. The Jews aren't going to buy any more Messerschmitts.

In the morning the weather front has passed and it is clear and bright and we prepare to take the midday train south. A communist parade is in the process of forming on the streets and a group of Russian officers are in the foyer of the Flora. Everyone ignores them. It is four blocks to the station and we take a taxi and from the windows we can see uniforms from everywhere in the Red Alliance. At the depot Lichter buys the tickets for Budejovice and we board one of the trains on the west end of the station. We are all dressed in sports jackets with open neck shirts and we all sit together on one wide seat. Lichter raises the window and leans out and, after the train pulls out, he sits back down next to Flint. The trip takes two hours and the car is full of people and at every stop they sell beer through the windows. We buy some beer and hold the paper cups on our laps. Lichter says that there were ten pilots in the previous group. They were American and South African volunteers. They left for Israel two days ago. Budejovice is not a large city nor is it essentially industrial. The farmland which surrounds the town stretches away to the hills and then to mountains and forests. The countryside is inclined to be picturesque. It is called Budweis in German and the airfield is a mile from the outskirts. We were to be at the Czech operational training base for three weeks.

We are issued Czech identification cards when we arrive and the same afternoon I fly with Lichter in the Arado. The flying suits and parachutes have Luftwaffe insignia on them but Lichter doesn't seem to notice it. He has been here before. I sit in the rear cockpit of the high-powered trainer and I experience a sense of uneasiness because the airspeed is indicated in unfamiliar kilometers and the altitude is registered in meters. The horizon suddenly slants to vertical and then it is inverted as Lichter takes the controls and performs a series of rolls. We come around to land from the unobstructed southern approach and we drop close above the single-seaters parked along the perimeter. We bounce lightly when we settle onto the wide flat surface of grass.

In the evening Lichter takes us around to see Colonel Hlodek who is the base commander. Hlodek isn't at his quarters, but outside the officers' barracks we encounter Captain Bilek. Bilek is the Czech instructor assigned to the Jewish contingent at Budejovice. He had served for five years with the Royal Air Force during the German occupation of his homeland. He is short with Slavic features and is apparently imperturbable. He laughs and says that most of the Czech officers speak English and he assures us that one of them will be in the control tower when we are airborne.

He is possessed of a disarming candor and he speaks freely about the present political situation. He says that he himself eased obediently into the communist fold because not to do so meant professional suicide with worse to come later. Colonel Hlodek lurches out of the latrine which adjoins the barracks buildings. When he sees us he smiles broadly and since he knows Lichter quite well he comes over and hugs him. Heavy set and red-faced, Hlodek has his blue tunic unbuttoned and he insists that we come into his quarters for vodka. Hlodek was a veteran of the Soviet Air Force but there is no mention of flying except that when we finish our drinks Captain Bilek says that we will check out in the Messerschmitt two-seater tomorrow.

The Israeli section was never referred to as such at Budejovice. It was not a clandestine operation but neither was it publicised and most of the Czech personnel treated it with studied nonchalance. They would not be obliged to do so much longer. Israel had purchased 25 of the Messerschmitt fighters and the last five were waiting at the factory field at Prag-Cakovice. Their delivery during July would conclude the first chapter in the story of an Air Force.

CHAPTER III

BUDEJOVICE

The Israeli Flight at Budejovice was now four aircraft. They are parked into the prevailing wind on the edge of the grass apron at the south perimeter. A path leads from the quarters at the officers' block of buildings, past the white-frame mess hall, along a row of elm trees and emerges onto the airfield at the western boundary where the slant-roof hangars face outward to the landing ground. Far across the field on the eastern border the huts of the Czech student pilots lie flat against the background of the distant meadows. A line of fighter planes squat impassively in front of the huts and along the utility road that runs to the forest at the north barrier.

Bilek is leaning against the side of the two-seater when I get out to the Israeli line. I wear the Luftwaffe flight suit again but Bilek has his parachute harness buckled over his uniform. He points to the nose of the Messerschmitt and indicates that this machine has a Daimler engine. We get into the cockpits and when we are strapped in I look back. The rear seat is so restricted that Bilek seems to be in a half-standing position. He looks over my shoulder and prompts me on the strange procedure. When I am ready Bilek motions to the mechanics who are by the leading edge of the port wing. They insert a heavy crank into the side of the engine cowling and begin winding the inertia starter. I watch them through the windscreen panel. The initial turns are difficult and both crewmen have to pull on the handle together but, as the momentum increases and the whining sound reaches a high pitch, one of them lets go while the other continues to rotate the crank with accelerating ferocity.

Bilek taps me on the back of the helmet and waves his other hand at the crewmen. When the mechanic disengages the handle I switch on the magnetos and press the starter button. The propeller begins to windmill and then the whirring of the inertia is obliterated by the blasts of the exhausts. I look through the canopy glass at the wing surfaces. The Czech national markings are bright against the mottled-grey camouflage. The wheel blocks are pulled away and we move forward, the exhaust popping and backfiring with the sound that is peculiar to the German engines and which was to become so familiar in the months ahead. The machine shudders and vibrates when the engine is revved on the boundary path and I stare for a moment at the quivering starboard wingtip. I turn to the instruments, tighten the throat microphone and call the tower on the radio. A green light flashes from the elevated wooden structure beyond the hangars. Bilek hasn't said anything on the cockpit intercom. I look behind and he adjusts the goggles on his forehead and nods. I check the elevator trim control on the left of the seat and open the throttle. The earth blurs beneath the wings and then we rise into the wide sky above the dark border of the forest.

It is two days before I fly the Messerschmitt fighter. For all the unfamiliar qualities of the two-seater, I don't have any undue trouble with it but both Bilek and Lichter recommend caution with the fighter. Because of the engine modification it has some unique desires. Officially called the Avia, the single-seater was in fact the German Messerschmitt 109G powered by a Junkers engine instead of the Daimler-Benz for which the aircraft was originally designed. This change necessitated the re-modelling of the installation mountings and the utilization of the broad-bladed wooden propeller. With these differences, and with the lesser horsepower, the machine was found to have high take-off and landing speeds, while the narrow gauge of the undercarriage, along with a monstrous torque, frequently caused dangerous direction deviations on the ground. The aircraft was considered worthy once airborne buts its potential for unmanageable behavior was indicated by the name Mezec (Mule) which was standardly applied to it.

The Messerschmitt is a short-range fighter. It holds less than 90 Imperial gallons of fuel and it has a flight endurance of something under two hours at a cruising speed of 310 kph. The Czech versions are armed with two 20mm cannon which are oddly underslung beneath each wing and two 7mm machine-guns are mounted along the engine, under the cowling panels, and are synchronized to fire through the propeller. Racks to accommodate 250kg bombs could be employed also and for all its other faults it was a formidable war machine.

There is a high, thin overcast and the wind has risen when I taxi the fighter the short distance to the take-off area. The safety belt and shoulder harness are tight and the odor of petrol is blended with the unsavory smell of the interior varnish which is vaguely reminiscent of the smell of decaying fruit. The cockpit beneath the square-cut canopy is narrow, compact, almost too small and the rudder pedals are on a line with ones' stomach. The seat is flush above the central fuel tank. I apply the brakes and stop the machine at the south marker. The extensive turf spreads away before me to the trees at the north end. Over to the left I see the activity around the maintenance hangar. I turn in the seat and look back through the canopy. The short grass is rippling in the wash of the propeller. Tiny white flowers are mingled with the grass. The leather helmet is too tight and I pull at it. Then the tower light blinks and I turn the Messerschmitt into the wind. The popping of the exhaust becomes a steady roar when I push the throttle forward and after a seemingly endless run on the ground, the machine gets into the air.

* * * * *

The clouds are lowering. After the midday meal we are in the quarters at the officers' barracks. The sauerkraut and dumplings and beer that we had for lunch have barely settled when we hear on Lichter's radio that the truce has fallen apart in Israel and fighting has started again along most of the fronts. We are lying on the cots in the big room and we hear the relay from the US Armed Forces Radio in Germany. Lichter and Flint sit up. The red-haired, sleepy-eyed Flint has a balled-up piece of notebook paper in his hand and he throws it toward a basket beyond Lichter's cot. It bounces off Lichter's head. Lichter doesn't smile. He gets up and goes close to the radio on the table in the center of the room and listens to the end of the report. He has been giving us our pay in Czech kronen and now he pulls a roll of bank notes from his pocket and holds some of them toward us. I sit up. After he gives us the money Lichter goes to the small four-paned window and looks out at the elm trees. Gusts of wind are swaying the branches. He says if it rains hard he is going up to Prague for a couple of days.

The weather is threatening when we get to the Flight line in the afternoon but I go up again in the fighter. Flint is having problems with the two-seater. He and Bilek take off ahead of me and when I am half-way down the run the fighter begins to swerve 45 degrees off course. The north boundary is looming closer and I push the rudder hard, like Bilek said, and the nose of the aircraft jolts back to center. In the air I stay below cloud base near the field and when I come in to land some raindrops bounce off the windscreen. I swerve again when I get on the ground but I catch it in time and then a crosswind carries the plane close to the students' line. I roll slowly back to the Israeli section and wonder if I'll like it in these machines. I watch the ground passing under the wing and memories of the other war come unbidden into my thoughts. It seems strange to be flying the Messerschmitts.

At four o'clock we are ready to take off on a two-plane formation flight. Lichter is in the other fighter and the sky to the north-east is ominous. We are preparing to start the engines when Lichter waves off the mission. A red light shines from the tower. The storm front is moving along the mountains and soon the rain falls across the summer fields. It drums hollowly on the wing surfaces of the aircraft and descends in slanting patterns onto the canopy. The wind increases in velocity and drifting sheets of moisture move steadily over the trees down the perimeter. Everything is suddenly wet. We run with our jackets over our heads toward the row of barrack buildings and the damp earth smells good.

The rain falls intermittently for two days and the fighters have to be grounded. We ride into Budejovice the first evening and Lichter takes the train up to Prague. I go with Flint to a cafe in the square and we have dinner. The beer is strong and afterward we go to another place and there is a violinist. No one speaks English. Flint leans across the table so that his face is close to mine. He says that he is afraid of the goddamn Messerschmitts. The violin plays and the rain falls and we can hear the thunder rolling above the sounds of the bistro.

At the end of the week the skies are clear again and when Lichter gets back from Prague the programme continues. The first day the surface of the field is soft and hazardous and some of the Czech students damage aircraft with ground loops during the afternoon. Lichter sends Flint to Bilek for more dual instruction in the two-seater and then we walk to the fighters. The horizon is pale beyond the forest. To the west I can see a long line of washing blowing in the wind at a distant farmhouse. I put on the parachute and get in the cockpit and close the heavy side-hinged canopy. A few yards to the right Lichter starts his engine and the noise is loud. I switch the radio on and the sound dims amid the crackling of the static in the helmet earphones. I work the fuel primer pump and the Messerschmitt rocks gently while the mechanics wind the inertia. The engine starts and the rhythmic rumbling creates a relaxing effect. I look over at Lichter and he moves forward from the line with rudder fishtailing. I turn out behind him and we take off into the bright air.

Lichter handles his machine deftly. We have a simulated dogfight at 10,000 feet and I watch as the patchwork of the earth below tilts diagonally. Then the wings of the aircraft in front flash upward and the windscreen is filled with the blue above. Lichter rolls while climbing, tightens the roll into a turn and drops out behind me. I smile to myself. It is two years since I have flown fighters. The propeller of Lichter's Messerschmitt throws off some vapor as he cuts across underneath. Beyond him, far below, the multi-colored fields merge with the hills and then disappear into the range of mountains. Lichter comes up off the port wing and gestures and we roll down together and, gathering speed, we pass quickly above the hilltop castle that looks down upon the town of Budejovice.

In the evening the clouds return and when we finish supper in the mess hall we go back to the quarters. The barracks seem dreary and the shaded overhead light leaves the corners of the room in shadow. Lichter goes out and when he comes back he says he was on the telephone to the Embassy in Prague. He takes off his jacket and throws it on the cot. He says the Jews have bombed Egypt with the three B-17s that were at Zatec.

It developed that sometime in June the enterprising Al Schwimmer had actually acquired four B-17s at a surplus field in Florida. Though stripped of armament and some of the instruments they were considered to be in fair flying condition and, because of the urgency which prevailed in the situation in Israel, they made plans to smuggle the bombers out of the States as quickly as possible. On 12 June three of the planes with volunteer flight crews were ready at Miami. The fourth had engine problems and after some delay it was decided to leave it behind. The others took off and, apparently without attracting attention, flew up to Millville. The New Jersey airfield had been used frequently in the covert transactions in May because there was no Customs authority at the facility and fuel could be bought for cash without official inquiry. The B-17s refuelled at Millville on the evening of the 12th. It was the first stop on a flight that took them over Greenland and around the British Isles and on down to Czechoslovakia. They completed the journey without mishap and after they arrived at Zatec the Jewish groundcrews began refitting the bombers and arming them with machine-guns on improvised mountings.

Ray Kurtz, an American Jew and a former squadron commander with the USAAF in Europe, was flown up from Israel on the Balak run to take charge of the operation. This operation was at first considered to be the relatively simple one of ferrying the B-17s out to Aqir but, when the ceasefire ended in July, orders were received to bomb Cairo en route. Though viewed by some as impulsive and vulnerable to international censure, the scheme was nevertheless welcomed with enthusiasm by the bomber crews. The aircraft, however, were far from ready for an actual combat mission. Of the three machines, only one had a bomb-sight and none of them had adequate oxygen systems. They were all provided with crude projectile releases and a collection of welding oxygen tanks. The replacements for missing instruments and parts were equally innovative. By the time the selected departure day arrived, the aircraft displayed such a lack of operational readiness that Kurtz almost aborted the project as too precarious. After a meeting in which the Jewish morale factor was weighed against everything else, they resolved to fly the mission despite the difficulties and uncertainty.

There was a final briefing at the Stalingrad Hotel in Zatec and then, on the afternoon of 14 July, the crews shook hands, embraced and then boarded the bombers for the flight into history. Most of them were from the original Miami group. The B-17s were loaded with the maximum capacity of fuel and bombs and they ran into trouble as soon as they were airborne. Right after take-off, Kurtz lost an engine in the lead machine but he was able to restore partial power to it from the cockpit. He was determined to continue the venture and he was still manipulating the carburetor/air mixture on the faulty engine when they flew into bad weather. The problems began to multiply after some of the flight instruments malfunctioned and, as they neared the Alps, the three planes lost sight of each other entirely in the heavy turbulent clouds. After fighting the controls for hours and maintaining contact with the others by radio, Kurtz finally got below the weather along the Albanian coast. Here they were fired on by suspicious anti-aircraft batteries and had to change course to the middle of the Adriatic. Nearly exhausted by flying through what seemed to an endless storm, the pilots emerged into clear skies over the Mediterranean and within the next hour were able to regroup the formation. They reached the Greek islands at dusk and Kurtz slid the side window open and waved goodbye. His B-17 was the only one going to Cairo. The other two would make bomb runs on Egyptian bases in the northern Sinai and the Gaza-Majdal area on their way into Aqir.

After the two trailing aircraft had turned away, Kurtz began to climb the B-17 up to the flight lanes used by the airlines going into Egypt. When they reached 25,000 feet the navigator fell unconscious over the chart table. Within minutes other crew members collapsed as Kurtz himself experienced a gathering blackness. He instinctly realized that the oxygen pressure from the substitute devices was inadequate for that altitude and he dived the plane back down to 13,000 feet. When the others had recovered from the effects of the thin air they all resorted to the emergency oxygen bottles which someone had the foresight to bring along on this strange odyssey. Kurtz regained the lost height but he didn't know whether the air supply in the small receptacles would last through the run over Cairo.

It was dark when they reached the North African coast a hundred miles west of the Nile Delta and everyone took their stations. Homing on the RAF Fayid radio beacon in the Suez Canal Zone they soon saw the lights of Cairo glowing on the horizon. The city was obviously unaware of their presence and Kurtz set the course on a line over the Farouk Royal Palace. The bombardier then took charge and, directing the B-17 onto the target, he released the cargo of high explosives. Kurtz felt the sudden rise when the machine became lighter and, pushing the nose down, he turned toward Israel as the detonations of the bombs began to light up the sky behind them. They landed at Aqir at 1030 on a clear evening.

The actual damage caused by the raid was comparatively small although 4,000 pounds of explosives had been dropped around the Abadin Palace in the Cairo affair. The psychological impact, however, was far reaching and was, in fact, of infinitely greater value than any physical destruction that could have been delivered by the B-17s at the time. Though it would not be recorded among the great feats of war, the mission was a valiant effort.

* * * * *

Lichter turns out the light and the room becomes dark and, lying on the cot, I think again of Israel and the beach at Tel Aviv. It seems long ago. The rains return sometime during the night. When the rain was heavy the grassy landing area would turn to mud and it was too dangerous to fly the Messerschmitts. We would lie on the cots in the barrack room and listen to the passing storm. A week passes before the sky is blue again.

Lichter says that I will be leaving for Prague tonight. I bank the Messerschmitt onto the final approach and, as usual, I have difficulty rolling the manually operated flaps all the way down. I stare at the handwheel that parallels the seat and pull on it again. The flaps drop another inch. Everyone wears a glove on the left hand in these machines to avoid blisters from this necessary but disconcerting task. The landing field is now large in the center of the windscreen and I begin to put back pressure on the control stick. I drift fast across the perimeter above the Israeli section and the tail starts to drop and I hold it off for a few seconds and then jolt onto the ground. Mud erupts and flies past the canopy and I try to keep the trajectory straight. Way down the field I turn off at an angle to the pine forest. The road that runs along the boundary is ridged with ruts that lead into pools of water.

At the southern line I shut off the engine. The canopy is open and I can see the groundcrew pointing to something at the north end of the take-off run. In the cockpit I lean to the left and look along the side of the cowling. One of the Czech student pilots has just become airborne and the Messerschmitt is hanging perpendicular to the turf a hundred feet in the air. Someone forgot to set their elevator trim forward. The scene seems frozen for an instant and then the aircraft falls off on one wing and hits the ground. There is a loud crack but there is no fire, no smoke, just a spray of mud and then a crumpled pile of metal. People start to run down the field. I stay in the cockpit and idly toy with the control stick. It was always a surprise that a life could end so easily.

Lichter and Flint accompany me to where the path turns onto the perimeter when I leave for Prague that evening. They are staying on at Budejovice for another week because so far Flint had proved particularly ungifted in handling the obstinate traits of the Messerschmitt. I carry the bag and we stop near the gate road. Lichter gives me some extra money for the train ticket and they turn and go back toward the barracks. They say that they will see me in Israel. I wait until they pass behind the elm trees and then I follow along the edge of the perimeter toward the main gate barricade. Bilek is coming down from the hangar and he crosses over by the Spitfire revetments and walks with me. We stop for a moment in front of one of the British fighters. There are five of them at this post and they were a gift from the RAF at the end of the war. Bilek smiles. He says that the Israelis want to buy them but the Czechs haven't agreed on a price yet. He raises his eyebrows. The sun has set and the sky is red and we walk on and talk about the winter in England and the

Spitfires in the snow. At the last revetment there is a soldier standing guard. To the side near the sandbags is something covered by a parachute panel. The center of the silk is bloodstained and muddy boots are sticking out at one end. Beneath this shroud is the body of the student pilot who was killed in the morning crash. The guard salutes as we pass. We walk down to the sentry post at the gate and I go over to the Czechoslovakian Air Force monument at the barrier and look at it one more time. The monument is an entire Messerschmitt set on top of a granite pedestal.

I ride the two miles to the railway station in a Czech service van that Bilek flags down for me, and it is after dark when the train gets into Prague. I go to a room in the Embassy section of the Flora again and when I walk down to the hotel bar I see Sam Pomeranz. The pleasant-faced American Jew is not only a good pilot but he is the chief Israeli engineering officer on the Czechoslovakian end of the operation. He beckons me over to a seat at the bar and we drink German schnapps. Pomeranz is stationed at Zatec but he is in Prague for the night and he laughs and tells me about Al Schwimmer. The airplane procuror is in Israel. After the B-17s left the States illegally, the Federal authorities closed in and Schwimmer had to abandon his business and everything else he owned and get out of the country. He left a day ahead of an indictment charging him with violating the Embargo Act.

I stay in Prague until the next evening and there is a rumor at the Embassy that the UN has arranged another ceasefire in Israel. By the time I leave for the train depot the rumor is confirmed. It is night when I arrive in Zatec.

At the small station a cloud of steam drifts from under the locomotive. Girls in summer dresses pass by. I walk outside and an Israeli technician from the base directs me to the Stalingrad Hotel. The obviously re-named hotel is down a narrow street a hundred yards from the station. It is old and not well lighted. It is the Headquarters for the Zebra operation. There is a cargo carrier crew at a table in the lobby and one of them arranges quarters for me. They are American Jews and I have some beer with them. They say that we won't leave for the south until morning. They know that I am from Budejovice and they talk about the recent fighting in Israel. The fighter squadron had been active since the truce was broken on 8 July. They had used the Messerschmitts as bombers and they had lost one of their pilots in action. Ground support missions had been flown against the Faluja pocket and there were other strikes that ranged from the Negev to Mishmar Ha'Yarden in the north. A volunteer American, Bob Vickman, was the pilot who had been killed and Mordecai Alon, the CO, had shot down an Egyptian Spitfire.

The C-46 crew start to talk about some of the action in early June – the time when only four of the Messerschmitts had been in service. A raid against the Egyptian Sinai base at El Arish had been organized but before they got off the ground it was cancelled and they were told to attack an enemy column which had advanced to a point along the coastal road, 20 miles south of Tel Aviv. The four, which included Mordecai Alon and Ezer Weizman, flew out to sea initially and then cut back in across the beach and strafed the Egyptians. Two of the aircraft were carrying wing bombs and though the strike was not extraordinarily devastating, the disruption that was caused succeeded in halting the advance. During the sweep, however, a South African volunteer, Eddie Cohen, was shot down and killed and Alon had to crash-land at Aqir. Eddie became the first fighter pilot in the Israeli Air Force to die in battle and on the one mission the newly appointed Fighter Command had lost half of its strength. The following day it was down to one aircraft when another Messerschmitt was lost near Natanya. This machine was hit by fire from an Iraqi armored force which was trying to push to the coast from Tulkarm. The pilot in this instance was an American volunteer named Rubenfeld who had since transferred from the Squadron. When he was forced to parachute from the out-of-control plane over the Jewish settlement of Kafr Vitkin, he had the presence of mind to shout loudly and persistently in Yiddish as he descended because the farmers in the area at the time considered anything in the air to be an enemy. As with many of the volunteers, Rubenfeld didn't speak Hebrew but his Yiddish served the purpose in this case because when he was picked up by an Israeli army unit the farmers hadn't hung him. The C-46 crew all laugh and they order more beer. Someone says that it was the day after this incident that Alon shot down the Dakotas with the one remaining Messerschmitt.

In the early morning we have coffee at the hotel and then ride to the base in one of the Czech military cars. The cargo carrier we are taking is on the flat concrete ramp by the main hangar. Inside the fuselage we have to squeeze between crates to get to the forward section. A Messerschmitt is lashed down on the starboard side and the disconnected wings are jammed tightly against the frame of the transport compartment. After what happened to the flight engineer at Aqir, I avoid sitting near the front bulkhead and I get up on top of some weapons boxes at the side of the narrow aisle. The pilot pushes through toward the cockpit. He says the crew I came up with are back in Israel. There have been changes since the month began. The Balak run has been closed down and the Israelis are using a different route. It is now called Operation Velveta and the fuelling stop is Yugoslavia.

It is sunny when we clear the end of the runway at Zatec and we turn on to the first leg which is a course almost directly south to Titograd. The Yugoslav airfield is not far from the coast of the Adriatic and when we land we find ourselves on a vast sod surface. There are mountains in the background and the C-46 lumbers across the field until we arrive at a number of frame buildings where we are met by the groundcrew. We have been in the air almost three hours. Many of the Yugoslavs are around the aircraft when we get out and most of them are attired in worn uniforms and some in under shirts. They begin the refuelling and they show evident curiosity about the Panama insignia. We stand around and watch the procedure for a few minutes. The system they are employing is crude in its simplicity because they merely pump the fuel by hand from large drums. A thin, middle-aged officer comes over and we follow him down a muddy lane until we get to a hut where they are serving food. We are offered a substantial soup and strong Yugoslavian liqor.

The Velveta route was not only more direct but it had become, a few weeks earlier, a pressing necessity for the continued delivery of military supplies to Israel. The United States, which remained single-minded in its belief that the Jewish-Arab conflict could be ended by the UN mediation, had put diplomatic pressure on the French to deny the Ajaccio stop to the Israel-based transports regardless of the Panamanian registry. The Panama ruse had been suspected in May during the early Schwimmer procurements but no significant action was taken until a month after the B-17 episode at Miami. With the Balak operation thus blocked at Corsica, an alternate refuelling base between Czechoslovakia and Israel suddenly took on an aspect of extreme urgency. The deal at Titograd was the alternative and it was another example of the Israeli ability to resolve quickly the emergencies that were commonplace throughout this war.

After a two hour delay because of ignition problems in one of the engines, we leave the Yugoslavian scene behind. The afternoon is fading and in three hours night falls outside the cargo space windows and the sea turns sombre below. Tel Aviv is easily discernible as we approach the coast of Israel but inland the lights disappear until the runway at Aqir comes into view. It is nearly the end of July.

The C-46 goes to the far side of a corrugated hangar on the south boundary and, when we get out of the aircraft and walk to the Operations hut, we can see one of the B-17s inside the maintenance compound. As soon as we go into the shack Bernstein comes through the field door. His face is browned and he looks different and his khakis are soiled. He smiles and says they are down at Aqir to change a cylinder head on the bomber. We sit down in some chairs in a corner and Bernstein talks. He says he likes Ramat David and that they [the B-17s] bombed Damascus during the fighting in July. Transportation is leaving for Tel Aviv and I stand up. Bernstein says that Sarah was the Israeli girl who was killed on the hospital plane in June.

CHAPTER IV

THE SQUADRON

I stay that night at the aircrew quarters in the Tel Aviv suburbs and when we get to the Beit Dagan crossroads on the way in from Aqir, two jackals run down ahead of us in the beams of the headlights. In the morning I am assigned to 101 Squadron at Herzliya. The Yarkon is the same and it is good to be there again. When I leave the posting office I get my kit and go across to the motor pool. Some people are climbing into the back of a truck and they say they are going to Lydda. I ask one of the volunteers about Bieberman. He says that Bieberman was sent back to the States two weeks ago because he was disconsolate all the time. I leave my kit at the motor pool and go out to the beach road and walk down past the Gallim Yam. I think of Bieberman and Sarah and the day we arrived in Haifa.

It is even hotter that it was in June and at the sea wall I stop and look out at the LST. Nothing had changed. It was rustier but the spray still flew over it and the water was shining beyond it like it always was. I go back to the cafe in Allenby Road. The cafe is dark inside after the brightness of the sun and someone calls to me from another table. It is Al Freeman. We had been together in the same US fighter group for a while in 1944 but I hadn't seen him after that. He comes over and, smiling, sits down. An easy-going American Jew, Freeman is with 101 Squadron but he says he has applied to go home since the recent ceasefire. He says he heard I was coming down from Budejovice.

Al Freeman arrived with the previous group at the end of June and went into action on 8 July when the first truce was broken. He laughs and says that everyone got bullet holes in their planes on the low-level missions and that one of the flight commanders shot his own propeller blades off when the machine-guns became unsynchronized. The greatest attrition to the aircraft, however, was caused by the accidents which occurred on the ground. Freemen talks about one of the Messerschmitts that went over on its back with a bomb under each wing. The pilot got a fractured skull but the bombs didn't explode because the detonators hadn't been set. He stretches his legs out beneath the table. He says that on the mission when Vickman was shot down there was a lot of ground fire at the time. Three girls come in and sit down at the next table. Two are wearing army skirts and the third a yellow-print dress. The one in the print dress smiles at Freeman. He gets up from the table. He says he will probably be leaving Israel tomorrow. He touches my shirt and then edges between the chairs and into the passage way. The girls smile and say shalom and he nods and then is gone out into the sunlight.

Herzliya in 1948 was an average Jewish town in Palestine. It had some cafes and small stores and a cinema and outlying houses with gardens. It is eight miles north of Tel Aviv and a mile from the sea. Beyond the houses, which date from the early Mandate years or before, are open fields. Many of the fields are cultivated but one, to the south of the settlement of Kafr Shmaryahu, is being graded into an airbase. Kafr Shmaryahu sits atop some grassy hills at the northern end of the strip and below lie the tents and stone block buildings of the base camp. To the east and south are groves of orange and fig trees. Cedars border the road toward town. The camp is the home of Israel's first fighter squadron.

When the lorry slows at the Command hut I jump down with the duffel bag and the truck continues along the road to the airfield. It is late afternoon and there are not many people about. Two girls watch from the doorway of the Communications shack. One of the girls has red hair. Modecai Alon is alone in the hut and he is writing at a desk that has scars in the dark wood. His bush shirt is clean and well ironed. To one side of the room is a leather-covered couch and behind a semi-curtained partition is a smaller room with a cot in it. Flies buzz sporadically through the doorless entrance. The sound is curiously restful. The CO doesn't ask any questions.

There are no aircraft at the Herzliya base. Everything is up at Natanya until the new strip is ready. The pilots return to quarters at Kafr Shmaryahu at nightfall. I follow the CO outside and one of the jeeps is coming down the dirt road from Herzliya. The road runs for a quarter of a mile through the southern groves and passes the administration huts and the mess hall, and then curves down to the operations area at the strip. The jeep stops near the Command hut. All of the occupants are either talking or laughing. A few have on light cotton flying suits but others are wearing tropical shorts and some are stripped to the waist. They are casual with the CO. He is addressed simply as Moddy. No rank, no salutes, no military stance. Laughter and curses, yet one gets the immediate impression that they know their job. The driver of the jeep is an imposing South African Jew and he gets out of the seat and comes over to where we are standing. Moddy says that the South African is the commander of B Flight. It is Sid Cohen.

From the heart of Johannesburg, Sid was in most ways a South African but as a Jew his desire to see a secure Jewish State in Israel was as strong, perhaps, as the similar desires of the most dedicated sabra.

When World War II began he was starting his medical studies which he forsook to enter military service and he was accepted early into the South African Air Force. Although he was large physically, he was appointed to fighters when he finished his training and was assigned to P-40 Kittyhawks in the Western Desert in early 1942. The Kittyhawks were the goats of the desert campaign and while attached to 4 SAAF Squadron, he participated in most of the North African battles that year and into 1943. By the time he finished his second operational tour it was 1944 and the Kittyhawks were obsolete. He was transferred to Spitfires and was beginning his third tour when the war finally came to an end while he was stationed in northern Italy.

Though not one of the spectacular fighter pilots which that era periodically produced, Sid had a unique combination of skill, endurance, and the ability to lead with an almost uncanny calmness of spirit. Like all who have seen action, he was effected by it but it was a mark that was rarely visible in the nature of him and he returned to civilian life with an attitude that was probably more outwardly serene than most. He, as was the case with any who flew in the great conflict, never forgot the air but he settled into the routine of making a living on the ground and he went back to his medical studies in Johannesburg. It was three years before he would again offer his services and, this time his experience, to a nation at war. Though he didn't arrive in the new State of Israel as early as did Boris Senior or Eddie Cohen, his unmatched qualities as a pilot and a leader precipitated his immediate appointment as a Flight commander in 101 Squadron after coming in from Budejovice in late June. To Sid, the fact that we were flying Messerschmitts seemed forever ironic and comical.

He looks different without a beard. At El Adem that autumn of 1942, Sid had a beard. I think of the night when we [members of 92 Squadron] were looking for the landing ground where the Spitfires were and the flat desolation of the Western Desert all seemed the same. We drove up to the mess tent of the South Africans. They were having a party. The South Africans always had brandy and it was the first time I met Sid. At two inches over six feet, he was at the tent flap with tin cups in his hands and he ordered us to have a drink. He called himself Cohen the Jew and he led everyone in singing ribald songs. We stayed there all night. Now we stand in the dust beside a stone hut in Israel and face each other again. The beard is gone but there is the same flat nose, the wide face, the calm eyes. Remembering, Sid takes my arm and we go over to the jeep and I meet the others. Sid Antin, Aaron Finkel, Sandy Jacobs, Giddy Lichtman. They joke among themselves. Then Moddy gets his jeep and we go up to Kafr Shmaryahu.

The winding, rutted road that travels up the hill from the camp turns on to tar pavement at the top of the rise, and then passes the scattered dwellings of the settlement and ends at a lane near the pilots' quarters.

White plaster buildings with red tile roofs stand back from the lane and a hedge leads to an entrance where there is a garden area with a large acacia tree by a screened dining hall. The rooms in the two wings of the pension buildings are small and to accommodate all of the personnel a sleeping tent had to be set up at the edge of the adjoining maize field. On the other side of the lane are the fenced corrals of a farm and, back where the tar surface terminates, there are a few houses and a store. Down behind a vineyard is a beer garden. On the northern side the dirt lane trails off to a deserted Palestinian Arab village and then the hills slope west to the open fields and the sea. Beyond the beer garden in Kafr Shmaryahu the main road continues for a mile and, at the junction where it bends toward Herzliya, there is a roadhouse. Below the roadhouse is the white sand of the beach that runs beneath the sharply-rising coastal escarpment.

Before dark the remaining pilots arrive from Natanya and after the evening meal everyone sits around in beach chairs under the tree. I go with Sid Cohen to the tent. He and the South African Arni Ruch are the only other occupants and, after I put my kit under one of the cots, we walk back out to the nearby garden. There are fifteen pilots plus the adjutant and engineering officer at the Kafr Shmaryahu quarters. When the last group from the auxiliary field comes in, the Gentile Chris Magee is with them. He has a red handkerchief on his head and a pistol on one leg and a trench-knife on the other. Like everyone else he is burned dark by the sun.

Moddy goes into Tel Aviv after dinner and Ezer Weizman gets the other jeep and we go down to the beer garden. Some are walking down and Ezer almost hits two of them when he spins the jeep on the dirt. Everyone curses and laughs. The night is warm and at the beer garden we sit outside under the lanterns which are strung overhead. The daughters of the proprietor serve the beer in glass pitchers and we drink and everyone talks. They talk mostly about the flying and I look at the faces and try to remember the names. Lou Lenart, an affable American volunteer who led some of the missions in the first days, is sitting next to Sid Cohen. Across the planked table are three others from the States – Bill Pomerantz [not to be confused with Sam Pomeranz], Leon Frankel and Rudy Augarten. Directly opposite is the A Flight commander, Maury Mann. Short, heavy and curly haired, Mann is an English Jew. Beside him there is another English Jew, the tall, relaxed Cyril Horowitz. At the front of the table is the happy American Stan Andrews, and the irrepressible Ezer Weizman.

The youngest of the three sabra pilots in 101 Squadron, Ezer is cultured and witty. Coming from a distinguished Russian emigré family, he is the nephew of the legendary Chaim Weizmann, Israel's first President. Ezer is possessed of both intellect and a sense of humor and his command of the English phrase is enviable, but beyond this it is his personal nature that serves him best. He has an obsessive dedication to the cause of the State but he also has the gift of approaching issues with an unshakable light-heartedness. Trained in World War II by the Royal Air Force, he attained the rank of Sergeant Pilot, which was almost the universal rank for the handful of Palestinian Jewish candidates who achieved pilot status with the British during those years. He served until 1946 and, although he never saw actual combat operations with the RAF and was less experienced than Remez or the brilliant organizer Dan Tolkowski or than Mordecai Alon, Ezer had already achieved the reputation of being one of the most flamboyant of the Messerschmitt pilots.

There are night insects circling about the lanterns and one of them flies into a beer pitcher. Sid Cohen says that it looked like one of Giddy's landings. Someone retrieves the moth and throws it into the bushes bordering the tables. Sid pours some more beer into his glass. He is the pilot who shot part of his propeller blades off on a mission to Faluja and someone jokes about it. Sid smiles and drinks his beer. Giddy comes over from the group at the other table. From Newark, New Jersey, he stands next to Ezer and, holding a glass, he starts talking about the time they were scrambled after some Egyptian Spitfires in June.

Everyone was in Tel Aviv that day because none of the Messerschmitts were close to being serviceable. In the afternoon Moddy was contacted at their town Headquarters in the Yarden Hotel and was told by HQ Operations to get two of his pilots and scramble. There were reports of the Spitfires fooling around along the coast south of Jaffa and three of the Messerschmitts at Aqir had suddenly and miraculously become combat-ready. The only problem was that the Jewish pilots were 20 miles away from the base. Moddy hung up the telephone and ran out of the room. The first two he encountered were Lou and Ezer. When they all got out to the street they discovered that Moddy's jeep was missing, which, although it was an annoying development, was not an uncommon occurrence in Tel Aviv during this phase of the war. Ignoring the stares of everyone on the walkway, the trio sprinted the few blocks to the motor pool at the Yarkon to requisition some transporation but here a clash ensued with the Duty Officer because they had no written authorisation. Out of breath, Moddy and Lou were angry and Ezer was infuriated. He ran into the middle of the road and flagged down an ancient taxi and they all jumped in the back and headed out of town. During the entire trip to Aqir, Ezer and the driver argued over how much the fare was going to be and when they got to the base they had to run another hundred yards to the Ops shack, where they found out that the scramble had been called off.

When Giddy finishes the story everyone laughs and Ezer smiles down at his beer glass. This incident, like so many others that became part of the legends of that year, tended to be embellished upon and exaggerated

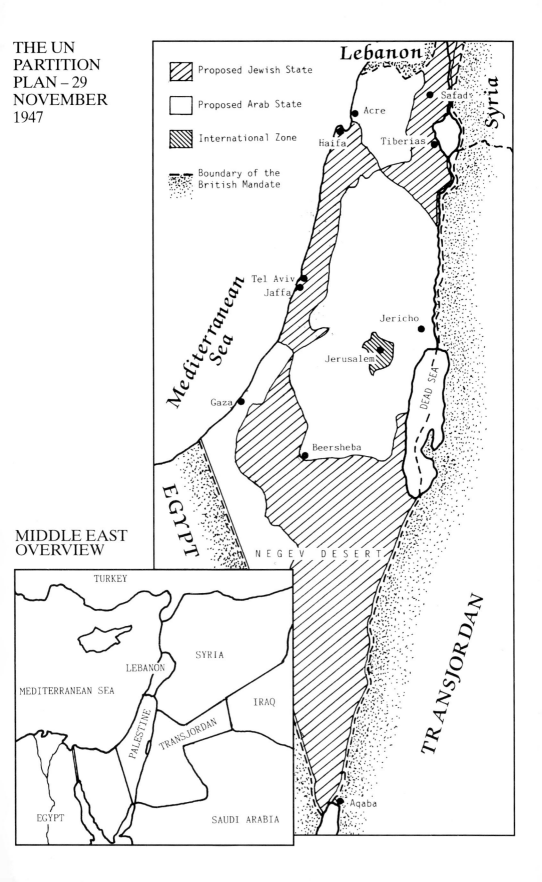

THE UN
PARTITION
PLAN – 29
NOVEMBER
1947

Proposed Jewish State

Proposed Arab State

International Zone

Boundary of the
British Mandate

Lebanon

Safad

Acre

Haifa

Tiberias

Mediterranean
Sea

Tel Aviv
Jaffa

Jericho

Jerusalem

DEAD SEA

Gaza

Beersheba

EGYPT

NEGEV DESERT

Syria

TRANSJORDAN

Aqaba

MIDDLE EAST
OVERVIEW

TURKEY

SYRIA

LEBANON

MEDITERRANEAN SEA

PALESTINE

IRAQ

TRANSJORDAN

EGYPT

SAUDI ARABIA

Newly commissioned Pilot Officer in the RAF; Leo as a RAF fighter pilot with 71 (Eagle) Squadron, 1942.

(Leo Nomis via NWMA collection)

Top: Leo posing with his 'own' Spitfire (BL287 XR-C) while serving with 71 (Eagle) Squadron, 1942.

(Leo Nomis via NWMA collection)

Above: With 229 Squadron RAF at Takali, Malta, August 1942. Leo is standing seventh from left. Seated in front of him is Wg Cdr John Thompson, Wing Commander (Flying) Takali, and on Thompson's left is Grp Capt Walter Churchill, who was killed in action two days after the photograph was taken.

(Leo Nomis via NWMA collection)

Left: Plt Off Leo Nomis (left) with Plt Off Art Roscoe, both 71 (Eagle) Squadron, 1942. *(Leo Nomis via NWMA collection)*

Top: The wreck of the ill-fated LST *Altalena* at Tel Aviv. (see pages 36-39)

Bottom left: A pilot with two hats: Leo after his transfer to the USAAF in 1943.

(Leo Nomis collection)

Bottom right: Leo in Israel, 1948.

(Leo Nomis collection)

Top: Messerschmitt D-107.
(Leo Nomis collection)

Above: 101 Squadron's first CO, Palestinian-born Moddy Alon (right) with American volunteers Lou Lenart (left) and Giddy Lichtman (centre).
(Giddy Lichtman collection)

Left: Left to right: Cyril Horowitz, Sandy Jacobs, Stan Andrews (killed in action 20 October 1948), Lou Lenart, unknown, Bob Vickman (killed in action 9 July 1948).
(Maurice Mann collection)

Top: The irrepressible Ezer Weizman (centre) with Bill Pomerantz (left) and Maury Mann (right).   *(Aaron Finkel collection via Shlomo Aloni)*

Bottom: Aaron Finkel and Sid Antin with Messerschmitt D-108.

(Aaron Finkel collection via Shlomo Aloni)

Top left: Sid Cohen, Giddy Lichtman, Moddy Alon, Ezer Weizman, Arni Ruch.
(Aaron Finkel collection via Shlomo Aloni)

Top right: Group of 101 Squadron pilots with Messerschmitt. On cowling, Maury Mann, Ezer Weizman, Red Finkel; on wing, Bill Pomerantz, Sandy Jacobs, Sid Antin; standing, Sid Cohen, Chris Magee, Giddy Lichtman, Leon Frankel, Leo Nomis.
(Giddy Lichtman collection)

Bottom: Same occasion, same group.
(Aaron Finkel collection via Shlomo Aloni)

Top: With the Squadron jeep at Ma'abarot, from left to right: Rudy Augarten, Cyril Horowitz, Red Finkel, Maury Mann, unknown, Leo Nomis, George Lichter.

(Aaron Finkel collection via Shlomo Aloni)

Bottom: Maury Mann and Sid Antin with Messerschmitt. *(Maurice Mann collection)*

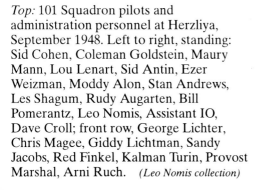

Top: 101 Squadron pilots and administration personnel at Herzliya, September 1948. Left to right, standing: Sid Cohen, Coleman Goldstein, Maury Mann, Lou Lenart, Sid Antin, Ezer Weizman, Moddy Alon, Stan Andrews, Les Shagum, Rudy Augarten, Bill Pomerantz, Leo Nomis, Assistant IO, Dave Croll; front row, George Lichter, Chris Magee, Giddy Lichtman, Sandy Jacobs, Red Finkel, Kalman Turin, Provost Marshal, Arni Ruch. *(Leo Nomis collection)*

Bottom left: Prime Minister Ben-Gurion's visit to Natanya. Left to right, Giddy Lichtman, Moddy Alon, David Ben-Gurion, Mrs Ben-Gurion, Maury Mann, Sandy Jacobs.

(Giddy Lichtman collection)

Bottom right: Ezer Weizman, proudly displaying his newly grown beard.

(Leon Frankel collection via Shlomo Aloni)

Top left: Giddy Lichtman poses in front of a Messerschmitt.

(Giddy Lichtman collection)

Top right: Cyril Horowitz survived a take-off crash in Messerschmitt D-122.

(Maurice Mann collection)

Bottom left: Maury Mann, Bill Pomerantz, Sid Antin. *(David Baron collection)*

Bottom right: Ready for action – Giddy Lichtman; he shot down an Egyptian Air Force Spitfire and an Arab Airways Dragon Rapide during his service with 101 Squadron. *(Giddy Lichtman collection)*

Top: Dragon Rapide TJ-AAE of Arab Airways, sister aircraft to that shot down by
Giddy Lichtman.   *(John Havers collection)*

Bottom: Leo Nomis and Cyril Horowitz at Falk's house, Kfar Shmaryahu.

(Leon Frankel collection via Shlomo Aloni)

Top: Bill Pomerantz in the cockpit of D-120. *(Leon Frankel collection via Shlomo Aloni)*

Bottom: Ezer Weizman tries to 'outdo' the image on the Squadron badge.

(Leon Frankel collection via Shlomo Aloni)

Top: 101 Squadron's Technical Officer Harry Axelrod in front of D-123.

(Leon Frankel collection via Shlomo Aloni)

Bottom: Debriefing at Herzliya (left to right) Ezer Weizman, Maury Mann, Sid Antin, Dave Croll (IO).

(Leon Frankel collection via Shlomo Aloni)

Top: Newly arrived Spitfire pilot Lee Sinclair (left) with Red Finkel and Messerschmitt displaying 101 Squadron's 'skull with batwings' badge.

(Aaron Finkel collection)

Above: Count Folke Bernadotte's UN-marked Dakota narrowly escaped becoming the victim of Messerschmitts flown by Giddy Lichtman and Leo Nomis. *(Al-Ahram Archive)*

Right: Maury Mann with the resurrected Spitfire D-130; while flying a Messerschmitt he shot down a Syrian Air Force Harvard.

(Maurice Mann collection)

Top: Messerschmitt D-120.

Middle left: Dov Ben Zvi, alias Baron Wiseberg, alias David Baron; a former Royal Navy Fleet Air Arm fighter pilot who flew a few operations with 101 Squadron early in the conflict.

(David Baron collection)

Bottom left: Moddy Alon, 101 Squadron's first CO who was killed when his Messerschmitt crashed on 16 October 1948.

(Leon Frankel collection via Shlomo Aloni)

Bottom right: Leo Nomis with Ezer Weizman in December 1986. Ezer Weizman commanded the Israeli Air Force from 1958 to 1966 and is currently (1998) the President of Israel. *(Leo Nomis collection)*

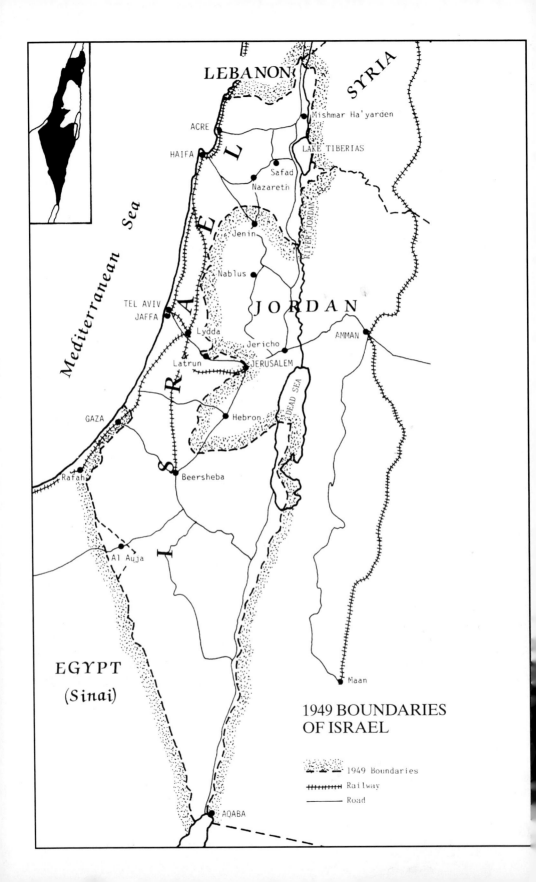

LEBANON

SYRIA

Mishmar Ha'yarden

ACRE

LAKE TIBERIAS

HAIFA

I

S

R

A

E

L

Safad

Nazareth

Jenin

Nablus

JORDAN

RIVER JORDAN

Mediterranean Sea

TEL AVIV

JAFFA

Lydda

Jericho

AMMAN

Latrun

JERUSALEM

GAZA

Hebron

DEAD SEA

Rafah

Beersheba

Al Auja

EGYPT

(Sinai)

Maan

1949 BOUNDARIES
OF ISRAEL

AQABA

······· 1949 Boundaries

++++++ Railway

———— Road

as time went on, and one version even had Ezer arriving at the base
directly from a bar mitzvah and scrambling after the Egyptians in a
tuxedo.

Giddy was one of the original group of foreign volunteers in the
Israeli Air Force. Twenty-five years of age, he was of medium height,
personable, cheerful and courageous. Arriving right after the
Declaration, he was in the second contingent at Budejovice and he was
at Aqir shortly after 101 Squadron was activated. He could handle the
Messerschmitts better than most and by the beginning of the second
month he had shot down one of the Egyptian Spitfires. The Jewish-Arab
war was a crusade as far as he was concerned and he wouldn't accept the
standard salary offered by the Agency to volunteers, receiving only the
subsistence pay that was alloted monthy in Israel. With the US 9th Air
Force in Europe as a P-51 pilot in 1945, he saw little action before World
War II ended but he had come to Israel to fight. The truces and ceasefires
annoyed him and during these periods he patrolled endlessly for the
elusive shufti kites and stunted high in the sun. Shufti kite (shufti, from
the Arabic word for 'look') was the popular term applied to those high-
level reconnaissance aircraft of unknown nationality that daily made
runs over Israeli territory. The quest to engage these seemingly
unreachable machines was seriously hampered by the absence of oxygen
equipment in the Messerschmitts, a situation that was mysteriously
never remedied during their entire length of service that year. The shufti
kites had been identified as British-built Mosquitos but the origin and
homeland of the rapid-travelling planes has yet to be established.

There is a half-moon in the cloudless sky when I walk with Sid Cohen
and Arni Ruch on the road back to our quarters. They talk in Afrikaans
sometimes and the jolly-natured Arni laughs at everything Sid says. Arni
isn't as big as Sid and he is fair-haired. He seems to be always smiling.
We near the lane and Sid is talking about when they got up to Italy in
1943 and he had met a girl in one of the villages outside Parma. She
wouldn't have anything to do with him romantically because she said he
looked like Jesus Christ. Sid says he shaved off the beard after that. Arni
laughs again and pulls at his tropical shorts. We turn through the garden
and walk past the white buildings. In the tent Sid lights a kerosene lamp
and our shadows appear large on the canvas. We get into the cots and roll
the insect nets down and Sid extinguishes the lamp. We are all sleeping
in our underwear. The voices from the buildings die away and the dogs
behind the dining hall stop barking and then there is silence and
darkness. A half hour later the jackals begin their wailing down the hill
and the chorus is answered along the line and carried far off into the
distance. The sound is like children crying in the night.

The morning at Natanya is clear and hot and a cloud of dust is
hanging in the air at the north end of the field where one of the fighters
is running up. Two miles to the west, beyond a line of cedars, the beach

town simmers by the sea. The trees continue across the southern edge of
the wide landing strip and turn back up the eastern side where they
separate the airfield from the inland road to Herzliya. The tents of the
groundcrew and the new covered aircraft revetments lie along the
perimeter to the north-east and, from a distance, they are distorted by the
heat devils which rise from the dry earth. The area is flat and there is a
perpetual crosswind. The approach from the north is directly over the big
fresh water vats of the fish farms. We had left Kafr Shmaryahu at dawn.
We could feel the heat of the coming day when we ate breakfast on the
screen porch of the dining room and then we got into the back of the
Squadron lorry. The ride to Natanya took 25 minutes. We were all
bunched together in the rear of the truck and everyone was quiet because
it was so early.

It is the first day of August and due to the ceasefire the flying at
Natanya is limited to line patrols; and futile attempts to intercept the
shufti kites. The cloud of dust on the north boundary is heavier now as
the single Messerschmitt swings around and, gaining speed, takes off
past us and roars down the strip. It lurches about but bounces into the air
farther along and barely clears the southern trees. Everyone turns their
backs to the rush of wind and we walk over to the Ops tent near the
maintenance area. I have been assigned to B Flight and Sid Cohen
arranges for me to go on a four-plane sector patrol. Giddy is appointed
to lead the formation and the others are Ezer and Sandy. The third of the
trio of sabra pilots in 101 Squadron, Sandy came over from the light
planes at Sde Dov and he has unsettlingly little fighter experience to be
flying the intolerant Messerschmitts. Small, almost frail, the
imperturbable Sandy is British-educated and speaks with the precise
intonation of the upper class but he says nothing now as we select
parachutes and gear from an assortment piled haphazardly on the floor
of the Ops tent. When we go back outside Sid unfolds a map on the
ground. He points to the salient created by the Partition and, indicating
that Tulkarm is the apex, he moves his finger along the approximate
positions of the Arab lines. He looks at Giddy and says that we will stay
away from them today. Tulkarm is eight miles due east of where we are
standing.

The Israeli and Arab positions along the fronts had changed little with
the comparatively brief fighting in July. In the diverse sectors the Galil
was still held securely against the Syrian attacks and the Alexandroni
Brigade had checked the Iraqis and Trans-Jordan Arabs in the west
salient. The problems with the Arab Legion in Jerusalem and along the
corridor supply route at Latrun remained and, because of the proximity
of the combatants in this situation, the area was forever involved in truce
violations. The Palestinian Arabs who had fled Israel's boundaries and
joined the invading armies were scattered generally among all of the
regular Arab forces, but they also had independent commands in the

salient and in the Negev to the south.

The major foe in the south was, of course, Egypt. This army had advanced into Israeli territory as far as Isdud, just north of what would become known as the Gaza Strip, and here they were stopped by the Jewish Givati and Negev Brigades and by the heroics of the people on the kibbutzes in their path. This latter Brigade also controlled the Egyptian forays to the eastern Negev and one unit, Chaim Bar Lev's 8th Palmach Regiment, proved to be particularly deadly in counter-attacking these enemy moves. Except for some advance patrol activity in earlier days, Isdud was to be the farthest penetration by the Egyptian ground forces and, as August arrived, their main invasion army was encamped there. Although they were halted, their presence was both morally and militarily intolerable to the Israelis, not the least of the reasons being that the airfield at Yasir (Hatzor) had to be abandoned because it was only two miles from the Egyptian artillery. To the extreme north, Lebanon had proved to be impotent from the first day and other than a rallying point for some of the Palestinian Arab groups it was considered neutralized. Lebanon, however, did provide a seaport for the Arab bloc countries which were landlocked and was looked upon during the war as more of an economic ally to the invaders than a military one. The situation as it stood on 1 August was far from being settled.

Ezer and Giddy are already in the cockpits and the shirtless crewmen are standing in the sun beside the planes when Sandy and I come out to where the four Messerschmitts are lined up. The mechanics are curious when I get there because they haven't seen me before. I climb onto the wing and the metal on the side of the cockpit burns my hand when I grasp the running edge for support. I stand on the wing and put on the helmet and fasten the parachute buckles. I look over at the Messerschmitts on the line. In contrast to the grey camouflage on those in Czechoslovakia, these are colored a solid pale tan with light blue under surfaces. The Star of David insignia on the fuselage is inordinately large and a thin blue and white band encircles the body in front of the tail section. Preceding the band is a Hebrew letter and a number in black. The Desert Hawks. As I get into the cockpit I look down the side at the number. It is 114.

We wait in the heat at the end of the field beyond the Ops tent. We wait with propellers turning idly for Sandy to pull into line. The inside of the cockpit becomes a furnace and perspiration drips onto the safety harness. The coolant temperature climbs to a dangerous point and Giddy comes on the radio and says we better get off the ground. Sandy swings around behind and when Giddy turns down field to take off, a hazy mist of dark smoke begins to come from Ezer's engine. It indicates an oil leak and he tuns in a wide circle and heads back to the maintenance area. Giddy signals with his hand that he is opening the throttle and I follow closely to his right so I won't be engulfed in the dust from his prop wash.

Sandy disappears behind us. We lift off near the south border and Giddy stays in a constant turn to the left. We come around low and parallel to the strip and then cut across so Sandy can catch up. The gear indicator light flickers and I check the handle. Everything seems all right and in a few seconds the light remains steady. When Sandy is in position on the port side, Giddy climbs to 9,000 feet and we can see scattered white clouds way off to the north. The cockpit is tolerable now as the cool upper air passes through vents.

Giddy takes the formation on a tour. Continuing north, Caesarea glides away under us on the coast and, across the narrow void between the aircraft, the illusion is created that we are all hanging suspended and motionless. We change course south of the Syrian-Lebanon frontier. The Israeli positions in the Galil string outward along the terrain and everything appears peaceful from above. We turn south over Lake Tiberius. Following the west bank of the Jordan River we come to where the salient cuts in sharply and Giddy clicks the R/T and points to the sector which is held by elements of the Carmeli Brigade. The lines are facing the ancient Jewish lands of Judea and Samaria and, down beyond Jenin, a veil of dust implies that there are troop movements by the Trans-Jordanians. We bank westward before we pass into enemy airspace and we are back on a course for the coast. Ramat David is off the starboard wing. We have been in the air for over an hour. When we approach Natanya we can see Tel Aviv clearly and away to the south-east lies sprawling Jerusalem.

Giddy has tired of the monotonous routine flying and he gestures for Sandy to change over. Sandy drops below us and comes up on my right wing. He is close in and the side engine panels of his aircraft are streaked with oil and dirt. As soon as we are in the echelon formation Giddy rolls down to the left. As I drop with him I can see Sandy from an inverted position for an instant and then ahead of me Giddy is rolling straight down at the earth. Kafr Yona is directly beneath us. The brown fields come closer and we pull up and the line of the sea passes by on the horizon. Giddy is rolling upward at the sky. I pressure the control stick strenuously. It is difficult to stay with him and the aircraft have become strung out. Sandy is now far below. After ten minutes of trying to catch up we come onto the approach at the Natanya strip and, one by one, make the turn over the fish farms and hold off into the crosswind when we land.

At noon a truck comes in from the Herzliya camp with lunch rations and we sit along the eastern row of cedars and eat sandwiches made of fig jam and rye bread. Giddy, Sid Cohen and Maury Mann are sitting side by side and Maury is talking about some problem he had with one of the machines during the morning. Someone is landing a Messerschmitt from the south because the wind has changed 30 degrees and we all watch as he settles and touches down on the strip. It is a good landing but then the aircraft suddenly swerves to the right and starts into a ground loop. The pilot is plainly using counter rudder but the Messerschmitt ignores it and begins to drag a wingtip. We stand up. One of the mechanics is urinating on a tree and he watches over his shoulder. The uncontrollable plane still has a lot of speed and it is now heading toward us at a rapid rate. No one moves and the only sound is the gunning of the engine. A billow of dust is streaming back from under the wing and as the machine's direction becomes apparent everyone on the line of cedars starts to run. Maury kicks over a tea mug that is on the ground in front of him and we begin to race toward the revetments down the perimeter. I look back and the mechanic is running behind us with his pants unbuttoned. The wayward Messerschmitt bears down relentlessly but before it gets to the perimeter it swings around to the west and one of the legs on the landing gear collapses. It comes to a stop 20 yards away, the wooden propeller churning the earth and throwing out giant splinters. The tail bounces six feet into the air and the engine dies. The dust settles and there is silence. Those who had been running come to a halt. Then, as is the case when one appears foolish in the face of danger, everyone laughs.

Moddy is at the Ops tent when we go back and his face is impassive. A Flight is sending out a two-plane line patrol and the tough, wiry, oft-times stoical Sid Antin and Red Finkel are gathering their equipment in the tent. They are both New York Jews and at thirty-two years of age they are the oldest pilots in the Squadron. Composed, sandy-haired, quiet, Finkel smiles to himself and carries his parachute toward the standby aircraft. I look at the maintenance board that is propped against the tent flap. There are nine Messerschmitts serviceable out of the fifteen at Natanya. Moddy tells Sid Cohen to bring me along and we walk over to a nearby revetment which, like the others, is covered from above by camouflage netting. The bright sun filters through the netting and onto a Spitfire which is suspended on wing jacks. Around the Spitfire are four mechanics and they are all wearing greasy shorts. None of them is wearing a shirt. Moddy calls the crew sergeant over and we go around and look at the engine. The aircraft is almost ready for operations. Moddy and Sid look under the eliptical wings and then go back and inspect the tail section. I stand next to Moishe the crew sergeant and look up at the nose spinner and then Moddy comes back to the front of the revetment. He nods to me and says the machine is an Egyptian Spitfire.

It was brought down in May, during the first week of the war. Hit by Bren gun fire on one of the Tel Aviv raids, the Spitfire was forced to belly-land north of Isdud and was captured by Israeli defense troops in the area. The pilot was taken prisoner and the machine transported first to the base at Aqir, where it was found to be repairable if enough replacement parts could be found. At the time there were discarded RAF maintenance supplies left by the British at Lydda, but whether or not there were enough miscellaneous Spitfire parts remained to be seen. A talented and industrious aircraft engineer, Freddie Ish-Shalom, took charge of the project of resurrecting the enemy plane and he and his mechanics began to comb the abandoned British depots for the essential material. They were soon directly aided in their search by the Egyptian fiasco at Ramat David which occurred shortly afterward.

In this incident, which many Israelis considered the most amusing of the war, the Royal Egyptian Air Force sent six Spitfires out from El Arish to attack the northern Palestine base at Ramat David, apparently without knowing that the airfield was still under RAF control. The Egyptians did some damage to the installation with the fighter-bombers and were on their way back across Israeli territory when Royal Air Force Spitfires caught up with them. The British pilots shot down five [sic] of the Egyptians and the wreckage was strewn across the plains. Most of the downed planes were demolished but one was salvageable after it made a crash-landing near the beach north of Natanya. Freddie Ish-Shalom would have his parts. Since the British, to a great extent, were supplying the Arabs in general and the Egyptians in particular with arms and aircraft, the Jews thought the episode not only funny but ironic. Moddy looks at the Spitfire which is now painted in Israeli Air Force colors. He says the Egyptian who crash-landed was a Squadron Leader [sic]*. He was the same pilot who had dropped a bomb on the main Tel Aviv post office in an earlier raid when 20 Jews had been killed.

In the afternoon I go on another flight with Giddy and this time Ezer accompanies us. After we rev the engines at the north approach, Giddy transmits on C channel of the R/T and asks if we are ready to go. Ezer is to the left of the undershoot warning marker and he sits high in the cockpit. He has on a cloth summer helmet and he holds an upward thumb toward Giddy. The R/T crackles again and Giddy, calling himself Blue Leader, contacts base radio. There is nothing resembling a control tower at the Natanya strip and base radio is a walkie-talkie device over near the Ops tent, where the operator has a Very pistol and a handful of red flares in case of an emergency. The range of the walkie-talkie is five miles and one quickly learned not to depend on it at any distance from the airfield. There is static on the control transmission and Giddy waves us on. He doesn't bother to give any unit call because we are the only ones on the frequency.

We are airborne and now we climb to the south until Tel Aviv is spreading out to the west of us. The sun is sinking lower and the rays flash a mirrored reflection from the canopies. At 12,000 feet Giddy turns east over Lydda. Ezer's Messerschmitt rises and falls in the clear air off Giddy's port wing. Ahead is Jerusalem. We hold the course and the city comes below us, bleached and majestic in the afternoon light. The Arab

---

* See *Spitfires over Israel* for further details of this incident.

lines run jaggedly across the Old City and the sun glints from the golden domes of the mosques. The dry, rocky hills roll away eastward and when we come around north of enemy-held Bethlehem, white anti-aircraft bursts blossom against the blue of the sky. They are some distance to the left, over Beit Jala, and Ezer dips a wing toward them. Giddy makes a profane remark on the R/T. We keep flying west and, far below, the railway line from the coast twists through the passes beside the corridor road. Southward, the Israeli outposts and settlements stretch across the arid Negev and we can see, away in the distance, where the Egyptians are stalled at Isdud. We pass above Aqir and Rehovot, south of Ramleh and Rishon-le-Zion, and go over the beach below Jaffa. Beneath the wings the sea replaces the varied colors of the land and we turn north and stay offshore because the Israeli fighters are restricted from flying over Tel Aviv unless engaged on an interception mission. When we pass Herzliya, Giddy peels downwards and light and shadow become blended as we slant in over Natanya. We go into the pattern singly and it is nearly dusk when we get on the ground. We are still in the cockpits at the revetments when a shufti kite buzzes above the airfield at 20,000 feet.

The early days of August pass slowly. The ceasefire remains in effect and everyone strengthens their position for the next round while the UN tries to negotiate a peaceful solution. Everyone knew there would be another round. In light of the situation three months earlier, the Israeli Air Force had made substantial strides. Though still operating under comparatively crude conditions and circumstances, the efforts of the Transport Group, the activating of a Bomber Command and the strong showing of the fighter squadron in the July operations, contributed immeasureably to the prestige of the young organization and to the spirit of the new State itself. The arrival of the Messerschmitts, regardless of their notoriety, had unquestionably changed the pattern of the war. Since the Dakota episode at Tel Aviv in June and the additional loss of some of their Spitfires to Israeli fighters, the Egyptains had, except for one unproductive naval sortie by two destroyers off Jaffa, relegated their raids to ineffectual night missions and strikes against isolated Negev settlements. The use of the Messerschmitts in an increased ground-support role the previous month had also created an adverse effect on the morale of the opposing armies but now, in the heat of midsummer, the fighters sat in the sun and waited.

101 Squadron countered the lack of combat activity during this period by continuing its efforts to intercept the shufti kites and by launching a photographic reconnaissance section. Military Intelligence at the Yarkon, which had only light planes from Sde Dov supplying them with limited information of enemy movements, had been anxious to have one of the fighters fitted with a camera. The captured Spitfire had already been tested by Boris Senior who, because of his abundant experience with this type, had come over to Natanya for the purpose. All had gone

well on the initial flight and with some minor adjustments it was considered operational by the end of the first week in August. It was designated as the PR aircraft. Dave Croll arrived from Intelligence and was assigned as the officer in charge of the reconnaissance operations. A heavy aerial camera was fitted into the vacant oxygen tank compartment behind the cockpit of the hybrid Spitfire and a hole was simply cut in the bottom of the fuselage to expose the lens. For several months the project would be known as the Spitfire Brigade.

To conserve fuel the Messerschmitts were assigned to alternating single-plane patrols and maximum-altitude flights were sent up for the shufti kite searches. The most dangerous part of these high-level missions without oxygen was the dependence upon the judgement and common sense of the pilot. There were no orders limiting the patrol altitude but anything beyond 18,000 feet was viewed as suicidal and everyone began to play a private game to see who could endure the highest climb. The Mosquitos were fast and they were probably lightly armed. Headquarters was inclined to believe that the RAF was conducting some of the sorties out of Cyprus and the Suez Canal Zone. Everything was theory until the intruders could be identified and orders came down to the fighter pilots to make every effort to ascertain the markings on the Mosquitos in lieu of shooting them down. Whatever their source, the shufti kites had acquired all the aspects of daytime phantoms.

CHAPTER V

A TIME IN THE SUN

It is the end of the week and I am on a two-plane patrol with Giddy. By ten in the morning we are out of the heat at 11,000 feet and 40 miles north of the base. We are turning west when we see a C-47 Dakota heading down from Haifa at 6,000 feet. Giddy doesn't say anything on the R/T and he slips downward so suddenly that I hesitate for an instant. Then we are in a steep, curving dive that brings the C-47 under us and I reach forward and adjust the gunsight. As the transport grows large in the windscreen I can see that it is white with big red UN letters on the wings and fuselage, but I stay with Giddy and wonder what he is going to do. Abruptly he pulls up and his voice comes in over the radio. He says we had better stand off. The Dakota is the personal aircraft of the UN Mediator, the Swedish Count Bernadotte. The sky is almost turquoise blue and we sit half a mile off the starboard wing of the Dakota as it heads into the salient toward Jerusalem. When we pass into Arab airspace, Giddy pulls his Messerschmitt over and flies upside down for a while.

Back at Natanya I stay under the partial shade of the netting at the revetment and talk to the groundcrew. Messerschmitt 108 bakes silently in the sun in front of the mechanics' tent and down the line Giddy takes his equipment toward the shade of the trees. Most of the groundcrew are either sabras or European Jews who came in at the time of the 1947 exodus, or before. They all smile and Isaac the sergeant hands me a canteen with warm water in it. The petrol truck pulls around in the dust and two of the mechanics go over to refuel 108. The machine is one which already has the new Squadron insignia on the engine panel above the exhaust stacks. The decal depicts a helmeted skull adorned with black bat-like wings imposed on a red circle. The design was principally the creation of Stan Andrews and the Squadron had voted unanimously to adopt it. Though it was totally devoid of any symbolic sentiment for the State of Israel, it seemed singularly apt to represent the undisciplined, war-scarred and unheralded collection of volunteers in Israel's first fighter squadron.

I look across at the insignia on 108. Isaac says that the aircraft has a
jinx on it. The others laugh. They say they have had a lot of trouble with
it and that it has already crashed once. They call it the 'Harlot' and say
that it is the one that killed the flight engineer on the C-46 at Aqir [this
was *not* however the aircraft involved in the accident].

The sun has dropped below the rim of the sea when the jeep leaves
for Kafr Shmaryahu. Sid Cohen is driving and there are six people in the
rear section. Harry Axelrod is talking about the hydraulic system on the
Messerschmitts. Harry is a volunteer from the States and he is the
Squadron Engineering Officer. He is a good engineering officer and the
burden of his job is unenviable. His facial expression is always serious.
Hydraulic failures have become a persistent problem plaguing the
maintenance crews, and Harry is telling everyone to operate the radiator
shutter control if a hydraulic lock occurs in the undercarriage system.
The resulting pressure reaction may unblock it. The jeep hits a rut on the
dirt road and jolts harshly upward. Harry continues to talk about his
theory. Everyone else is talking at the same time.

At the pilots' quarters there is boiled chicken for the evening meal.
Sid Cohen and Arni Ruch go to the water spiggot near the tent and wash
for dinner while others wait to get into the single latrine and the shower
behind the porch. Considering the demands and restrictions of the war,
life at Kafr Shmaryahu was comfortable that summer of 1948. When the
operational duty was alternated between the two Flights those who
remained at the quarters would go down to the beach beyond the
roadhouse. The days were sunny and at the beach the wind was warm
and the water was clear. You could see down where the sun made
patterns on the sand of the sea floor. Sometimes the girls from
Communications would come over from the camp at Herzliya and we
would have drinks at the roadhouse on the way back in the evening. In
the tent we change our shirts and then walk out to the screen porch. Mr
Falk serves the chicken. Kindly and white-haired, he owns the pension
house.

B Flight is off in the morning and when Moddy comes by in his jeep
some of the pilots are sitting in the chairs under the acacia tree. Moddy
calls Ezer over and then motions to me. When we get to the jeep he says
we are going to see the commander of the army camp on the plateau
north-west of Kafr Shmaryahu. He doesn't say why he is going there or
why he wants us to accompany him. I sit in the back of the jeep and the
breeze is in my face. We go down the tar road. Ezer is speaking in
Hebrew and Moddy stares straight ahead. We are all wearing British
desert shirts.

Moddy is the oldest of the sabra fighter pilots at 28 years of age. Like
Ezer and Aharon Remez and others, he had been a Palestine volunteer
with the Royal Air Force in World War II and he emerged as a Sergeant
Pilot during the last year of the conflict. He and Ezer had taken their

initial training together in Rhodesia but when they were assigned to fighter school, Ezer went on to the American-built Thunderbolts and eventually sat out the war at a base in India, while Moddy was designated for Spitfires. The war ended before he saw much action with the RAF, however, and he returned to Palestine to be demobilized and to find the smoldering friction between the Jews and the British, and the Palestinian Arabs and their allies of the Arab Bloc irregulars, ready to ignite. By 1947 he, along with the other native Jews with aviation experience, was engaged in what was known as 'underground flying'.

The situation at the time was that both Arab and Jew were unhappy with the pending Partition of Palestine and the British, who were in many ways responsible for the dissatisfaction, particularly where the Jews were concerned, were still officially in control of the country and were, in effect, in the middle. They had then thrown the future of the Jewish homeland into the lap of the UN. As the Security Council struggled with the Partition problem, the position of the adversaries worsened. Jewish settlements, especially those which were somewhat isolated, became in constant danger of hit and run attacks by the Palestinian Arabs and the irregulars, and the Haganah Palmach and IZL began to retaliate. Blood was spilling during the entire year before the Mandate ended.

In order to obtain aerial reconnaissance of these enemies and to maintain contact with the scattered Jewish underground forces, the small number of sport aircraft available to the Jews were secretly put into service. These mainly originated from Sde Dov where they were assigned to various areas. Ezer spent nine months in the Negev during this period, flying an Auster and co-operating with the recently formed Palmach units, while Moddy was with the Galil Flight in the north. At the end of April 1948 they were summoned by the Haganah leaders to a clandestine meeting in Tel Aviv and told of the Messerschmitt deal in Czechoslovakia. It was agreed at this meeting that the fighters be given the utmost priority and Ezer and Moddy plus three foreign volunteers were despatched to Budejovice. They arrived in Czechoslovakia the first week in May and three weeks later, in Israel, 101 Squadron was formed. Moddy was not immediately appointed as CO of this first squadron in the Israeli Air Force and early missions were led by the more experienced foreign volunteers, but after the destruction of the Egyptian bombers at Tel Aviv he became the unanimous choice for the CO, as well as the best known hero in Israel. Modest and introverted, fame didn't seem to mean that much to Moddy and he placed duty and final victory above popularity. Although he had little previous experience as a leader, he managed the Squadron with energy, wisdom and patience but no one was really close to him.

At the army camp we have tea with the commander in the officers' mess and he and Moddy talk for a while in Hebrew and then we all go out to the firing range. There is no shade. Some of the soldiers are testing one of the Czech machine-guns. They are using sandbags set against a rocky embankment as targets and we watch until the bullets have torn the bags to shreds. The commander smiles. He walks with us out to the jeep. He has a waxed moustache and his tropical shorts have a neat crease in them. On the way to Herzliya, Ezer inclines his head toward the back seat and tells me the reason for the visit to the army camp. He says Ben-Gurion is going to be at Natanya in two days and the army will supply some of the guards. It is never explained why I was invited on the trip.

At noon the next day I go on a shufti kite patrol. Leon Frankel, the black-haired, ex-US Navy pilot from Milwaukee has just landed. He says he saw nothing. When I get into the air I turn north and keep climbing until the altimeter needle passes 15,000 feet. I experience periodic sighing intakes of breath but I hold altitude and patrol for an hour on the line between Natanya and the outskirts of Haifa. I look upward most of the time and the brilliance of the sun creates dancing circles of light when I look away. The Mediterranean sun. I look around. The sky is vacant for a thousand miles.

In the afternoon I take Messerschmitt 113 on a test flight. 113 has just come out of maintenance and it is another machine considered to be an arch trouble-maker. It has been crashed twice and has a history of countless mechanical malfunctions. They call this one 'The Bastard'. After I run up the engine and check the instruments I turn up wind and it gets off the ground smoothly and continues to perform well during the half-hour flight. When I bring it back in the landing is not a good one and the Messerschmitt takes instant advantage of it by ground looping. Fortunately the wingtip stays clear of the dirt and the field to the right is open because I am unable to come to a stop until I am over by the western cedars. I sit facing down wind and my shirt is saturated with sweat. At the north end of the strip another Messerschmitt is taking off.

During this summer 101 Squadron was, in fact, an international squadron. The vast majority of the pilots were of Jewish origin but they had all served in the forces of other countries and none but the sabras were on their native soil. Emerging from the turbulent years of World War II, they had something in common from the past but what they had in common now was their belief in a Jewish victory. Discussions among this rather extraordinary group could be found in progress at Kafr Shmaryahu any evening after the sun went down, and one of the places where they gathered was the roadhouse.

The roadhouse is a bistro/cafe with a dance floor and porticos that lead out to a terrace. It has a tan stucco exterior and you can hear the sound of the surf from the outside tables. One night we arrive in a single jeep and we take drinks from the bar out to the terrace. Sid Antin winds up the gramophone near the wall and looks through a pile of records. All of the records are old and Sid Cohen wants 'Beyond the Blue Horizon', but Antin can't find it and he puts something else on. At the tables they talk about operations, about when the fighting will start again, about the aircraft, about the politics of the war. The complexities of the policies, both domestic and external, involving Israel at this stage is a subject regularly debated and an absolute master in this category is Ezer. They talk about politics now but Ezer ignores the issue for the moment. Reclining in a wicker chair and holding a glass of cognac he pulls at the light, sparse beard on his chin. He smiles at a thought which has occurred to him and tells everyone to shut up about political bonds. He says the strongest bond in the Squadron is the collective desire to survive the Messerschmitts.

At eight o'clock in the morning the entire Squadron is assembled at Natanya. The Prime Minister isn't due until ten and we sit near the trees and try to stay out of the sun. There is one plane up on a patrol but everyone else is waiting for Ben-Gurion. Nothing has changed. No one is dressed differently except Moddy, who has added a wide, webbed British service belt to his regular attire. None of the aircraft are lined up in show formation and they remain scattered about the airfield at the dispersal points. Most of the groundcrew have their shirts off as usual. The guards from the army camp are lounging near the revetments. Everyone is perspiring by the time the two Rapides come in from Sde Dov and taxi over to the eastern border. Ben-Gurion, with his prominent array of cotton-like hair gets out of the first one, accompanied by his wife who is holding a purse with exceptionally long straps on it. They are officially greeted by Moddy and, of those in the surrounding group, many are taking photographs. Moddy and the escort show the party to a jeep and they go on a short tour of the perimeter. When they return the pilots are introduced. There is shouting and jostling and laughter and we all feel suddenly honored shaking the hand of the illustrious leader about whom we had heard so much. Everyone is milling about when a shufti kite appears high overhead, a tiny speck against the wisps of cirrus clouds that are streaked across the deep blue above. The patrol aircraft had landed before the Rapides came in and everyone just looks upward and watches the intruder plane.

B Flight is on standby and Sid Cohen looks over at Moddy to see what he is going to do. Ben-Gurion, wearing dark slacks and a white summer shirt, is also looking at the sky, shading his eyes with his hand. Abruptly, Moddy tells Sid to scramble four planes. Sid points to me and grabs Giddy by the arm and shouts to Bill Pomerantz. We start running to the nearby readiness jeep and jump in. Sid floors the throttle pedal when the motor starts. We head for the revetments. The rotund Pomerantz smiles sceptically as we watch the shufti kite fast disappearing to the north. Everyone knows it is futile to scramble and when we get to the standby Messerschmitts, Moddy cancels it. A red flare arches up from behind the Ops tent and falls to earth out on the field, where it burns and sputters for a moment. The gesture for the Prime Minister has been made. An hour later Ben-Gurion leaves Natanya and the Rapides lift off slowly in the midday sun.

The strip at Herzliya is nearly ready by the middle of August but we are still at Natanya. George Lichter and Red Flint come in from Czechoslovakia and a few days afterward Flint wrecks one of the machines while landing. Moddy sends him down to Sde Dov. The veteran Lou Lenart is tired of fighting the Messerschmitts and he goes to a desk job at the Yarkon. The ungracious Desert Hawks continue to take their toll of the pilots as, in turn, Stan Andrews is sent to Ramat David to fly the Beaufighter they have procured somewhere. Lichter is going back to a European assignment in a week and he stays temporarily in the tent with us. There are no more Messerschmitts coming in from Czechoslovakia but Lichter says they are trying to make a deal for Spitfires. We all smile but Lichter looks unelated. He says the Czechs want a hell of a lot of money for them. Before he leaves Israel, Lichter puts on an admirable display of aerobatics in the clear morning air at Natanya.

On a weekend when a section of each Flight is off duty we go down to the beach. We take the jeep and Sid Antin goes across the lane to the farm corral and borrows the white horse, Gebor, and rides him bareback down the hill. At the beach some of the Communications girls from camp are there on the sand and Sid Antin gallops Gebor past them to the tide swirls and the hooves throw water high in the air. We wear our khaki shorts and we go into the surf. It is cool and everyone shouts. When we come out of the water Giddy lies down on the sand next to Leni. All of the girls are pretty and Leni is the smallest and she and Ruth have dark hair. The one with red hair is Miriam and she is married. Her husband is with the army in the Galil. I lay down on the warm sand too. To the north I can see the empty beach stretching into the distance beneath the bluffs of the plateau. We stay there most of the day and late in the afternoon someone in a Messerschmitt comes low along the surf line. The propeller is barely missing the tops of the waves.

The Spitfire Brigade is activated during the second week of the month and it is decided that only those who have experience on the type will be assigned to it. The names are written on the blackboard at the Ops tent and mine is on it, along with Sid Cohen, Moddy, Maury Mann and Arni Ruch. The photo reconnaissance missions begin with Moddy taking the first sortie in the Jewish shufti kite. It is mid-morning and I go with Sid Cohen over to the Spitfire revetment where Moddy is talking with Dave Croll. We look underneath the aircraft and see where the camera is lined up with the opening. We walk around in front and Moddy and Croll have a map spread out under the wing and Croll is indicating an area with a pencil. He is a bespectacled American Jew, young and conscientious about his job. He makes the trip into the Yarkon with the films each time the missions are completed. Moddy folds the map a certain way and climbs into the cockpit of the Spitfire. When he starts the engine it fires smoothly and we all stand back from the blast of the propeller wash. The cockpit canopy has been removed like they were on the Spitfires in the Western Desert and the Star of David emblem on the fuselage of this machine is so large it laps over the top. Moddy taxies out, stops near the boundary and turns the Spitfire around. After a moment he nods over to us and opens the throttle.

The following day I go on one of the reconnaissance flights. I sit in the cockpit for a while before the mission and my thoughts return automatically to 1943, the last Spitfire I had flown and the plains of North Africa. Croll jumps up on the wing, bends over the seat and explains the camera operation. It is an uncomplicated procedure with a switch box on the right-hand side of the cockpit and when the switch is on a small green light flashes for each exposed frame in the camera. The section to be photographed is circled in pencil on the map attached to a clipboard beneath the instrument panel. The circle surrounds an obscure sector on the edge of the salient eight miles west of the Jordan River. Croll gets down from the wing. It is almost noon and the smell of exhaust fumes and hot oil is heavy in the air. I look over at the mechanics standing to one side and resembling, for all the world, the crew of a pirate ship. I think of the labor in the sun that was necessary to resurrect the Egyptian machine for service with the Israeli Air Force. I look at them and the others in the far revetments, sweating over the Messerschmitts, and I am reminded of the unsung heroes in this war. I start the engine.

Croll wants the run at 8,000 feet and when I get to the target vicinity there are some billows of white clouds at the same altitude. The Spitfire handles well and I drop down 500 feet to clear the base of the clouds and begin the camera run from west to east. There is nothing visible on the terrain below to suggest that there is anything of importance along the course. Some of the fields in the area are green from irrigation and there are dissecting roads and junctions at various angles. To the left, in Israeli territory, Nazareth seems complacent in the sun. Below there is no movement. There is little concern for enemy fighters on these sorties but I look around at intervals during the run. It is necessary to fly relatively steady while the camera is operating and, as the seconds tick by, one becomes curiously aware that one is intruding on someone's property. I finish the first segment and turn onto the reciprocal course and use up the film coming back across and then turn south-west toward Natanya. When I land at the strip the Spitfire floats lightly in the ground thermals before the wheels touch the dust.

We soon find that the reconnaissance missions cause the Arabs to complain each time about truce violations and it amuses us because both sides are engaged in the practice. The Israelis, in turn, report the shufti kite incursions and the UN observers take note of the complaints.

The resulting success of the Spitfire Brigade during the remainder of August so impressed Military Intelligence that Headquarters requested additional PR aircraft from the fighters and two of the Messerschmitts were subsequently modified to carry cameras. By September most of the pilots in 101 Squadron were periodically engaged in these flights and the Yarkon became ever more ambitious in ordering missions which strayed far into enemy territory. The energetic Croll does not always divulge what they are looking for when he gives the map reference and course for the runs, but the day after the northern mission he shows me prints of the photographs and say they discovered a recently reinforced enemy artillery position.

It is late August and I walk with Sid Cohen to the tent at Kafr Shmaryahu. The afternoon is waning and we are off duty for the day. The side flaps of the tent are rolled up but the air inside is warm and we remove our shirts and lie down on the cots. Sid takes his high-top desert shoes off and we get under the nets to escape the harassment of the flies and we talk about the war. This war. Sid discards his normally casual manner for a moment. He says that if he survives up here and if, in the end, the Jews are guaranteed their national homeland, he is going back to university in Johannesburg and complete his degree in medicine. He leans on his elbows beneath the transparent, curtain-like net and looks out to where the sun is bright on the white walls of the pension buildings. He says that the Jews need a decisive military victory, not just a moral one. Then, maybe, there will be hope for some kind of peace in the future. After a pause, he gets up from the cot and goes outside to the faucet for a drink of water. When he comes back he sits on the edge of his bed and says that the UN mediation isn't going to really solve it. He says that Bernadotte is weakening toward Arab demands and the only way the Jews are going to get what they want is to fight for it. I listen and what he says is something that we all already know. He picks up a piece of paper and a pencil from the top of an ammunition box at the foot of the cot and, using the surface of the box to write on, he makes out the flight schedule for the next day.

Sometimes at night a party developed in Falk's garden. On one of these occasions a plank has been placed atop two empty fuel drums, and bottles of beer and cognac and seltzer are placed on the plank and everyone serves themselves in the middle of the yard. Moddy, who doesn't drink much and usually stays in Herzliya after dark, comes over for a while and by ten o'clock everyone but he is drunk. There is a full moon and we all sit beside the porch. Down the slope, moonlight is shining on the sea. Voices gain in volume when an argument starts over whether the Americans are the better pilots in the Squadron. Moddy watches with a mechanical smile. Someone starts telling the story about the time they had the party at the Yarden Hotel in Ben Yehuda Street to celebrate Rubenfeld's deliverance from the hands of the farmers of Kafr

Vitkin. Moddy didn't drink much that night either but the others who were present did and, although their quarters were in the Yarden at that time, everyone got to bed late. In the morning Ezer missed the jeep to Aqir and the only other transportation we could find after he woke up was Moddy's motor bike. He leapt on this machine and was roaring past the junction at Beit Dagan when he hit a mortar shell hole and went over the handle bars. He missed a week of the war and even more regretfully missed the Dakota incident which occurred while his wrist was being put in a cast at Tel Aviv's Hadassah Hospital.

There is laughter and the talking gets louder. A discussion is on about what would have happened if Marcus hadn't been shot. Colonel Marcus, an American Jew and an expert military strategist, was killed in Jerusalem in early June. An excellent officer, he was a graduate of West Point and he had compiled a distinguished record in the US Army in World War II. He had resigned his commission in the States to serve in Israel and he had originally arrived in Palestine in the first months of 1948, under the name of Stone. A skilled organizer, Marcus was not only an asset to the army command of the time, he was also involved in arranging the Messerschmitt deal in Czechoslovakia in March. Great hopes were pinned on his leadership abilities by the Israelis and he was considered one of the most valued of the foreign volunteers. Fate had ended all the plans that night in Jerusalem. The original version was that Marcus was killed by a sniper bullet near the ramparts of the Old City in the darkness before dawn, but the official revised account, which was released a few days later, stated that Marcus was shot by a Jewish sentry who mistook him for an enemy in the dark.

Moddy finishes his drink under the acacia tree and, waving a hand, goes out to where his jeep is parked beside the hedge. The headlights flash fleetingly across the yard as he leaves. When he is gone everyone exhorts Ezer to do his dance. Some of the pilots had been throwing beer at each other and everybody is wet. Ezer takes off his saturated khakis and in only his underwear begins cavorting and whirling through the garden in the moonlight, the gyrations of his tall, lanky figure accompanied by shouts and laughter.

At the end of August the operations are finally moved to Herzliya. Everything is packed up and brought out of Natanya and the aircraft are flown to the other strip. When Giddy and I bring out two of the Messerschmitts it is nearly deserted at Natanya. Papers and debris blow across the space where the revetments had been. We take off and bank back around and the hot wind trails the dust over the empty field. We pass above Khalid behind Natanya and see the lorries turning onto the south road.

The landing area at the Herzliya camp has been completed except for furrows of soil along the boundaries. We come in low over the orange groves and land from the south and bump down to the end of the dirt strip to where the hill rises up to Kafr Shmaryahu. The dispersal section is near the trees at the southern border and to the west side of the perimeter. The Squadron administration has been operating at Herzliya since July and, after we park the Messerschmitts at the grove revetments, we leave our gear and walk along the dusty trail that goes across 50 yards of cracked, dry ground to where the stone block huts are grouped. The mess hall is the largest of these buildings and it sits on a slight rise opposite the Squadron orderly huts. We go in and have the noon meal of lentil stew. There is an alternate meal of lesser substance for the orthodox who question the origin of the meat in the stew. Everyone on the base eats here at midday and we see Leni and Ruth at one of the board tables in the rear of the hall. Leni comes over and talks with Giddy while we eat. When Ruth passes the table on her way out Leni goes with her. We finish the meal and take the tin plates up to the kitchen section and go back outside. Some Palestinian Arab prisoners of war are working on the road that passes by the huts and an army guard, with a Mauser rifle slung on his shoulder, is standing to the right of those who are laboring with shovels. The guard is in his teens and is talking with a grey-haired, middle-aged Arab. The guard smiles when he sees us and we go over. He nods toward the Arab and says, first in Hebrew and then in English, that the Arab's name is Abbas and that he is the chief of the labor gang. Abbas is brown and sinewy and his clothes are covered with dust. He has a winning manner about him and he speaks English well. He says he was born ten miles from Herzliya and has many Jewish friends. We offer him a cigarette and he smiles and lights it. He watches us carefully when we walk down the road to the Ops tent on the fringe of the grove.

CHAPTER VI

HERZLIYA

That afternoon at the base camp strip I fly the northern shufti kite patrol. The control tower is still under construction but the ground radio is more sophisticated than that which we had at Natanya, and I call in over the R/T as Blue One. I am in 115 and they had to wind it twice before it started. The crew has sweated and cursed. It is imperative to get into the air quickly to avoid overheating the engine but Rudy Augarten, who is taking the patrol south of the salient, has just gone down the field and I can't see anything until the dust clears. I hear Rudy on the R/T and he says Red One is airborne and after a minute the dust drifts away from the strip and I start forward. Every time I take off in the Messerschmitts the same three words from a war verse enter my mind – 'Forward and farewell'. The wind sock near the tower shows a slight breeze from the north-west and the aircraft runs its usual length on the ground before it departs into the air. The hill at the boundary seems deceptively close when I pass above Kafr Shmaryahu. I look down and I see Gebor in the farmyard below.

The sky is absolutely clear. The tachometer is fluctuating as I climb but I have learned not to worry about anything on the Messerschmitts unless it is a total malfunction. I level off north of Caesarea at 16,500 feet. I look at the altimeter for a minute and climb again until it reads 18,000 feet. I feel altogether uncomfortable and the height without oxygen gives rise to a certain amount of anxiety, but I remain at 18,000 feet and patrol in a crossing pattern toward Haifa. I stay up sun as much as possible and on one of the inland turns I can see Red One banking away south of Tulkarm. When I am going into the sun's radiance for the third time I glimpse a dot high to the left. Below, Haifa is off the starboard wing and I turn sharply outward. The maneuver brings the Messerschmitt about at a flight angle to the dot which has rapidly enlarged. It is a Mosquito and it is either oblivious or contemptuous of my presence. The course it is following is directly across the path of the Messerschmitt and 5,000 feet above. The dark underside of the shufti kite doesn't reflect much light in the bright air and it is moving at a fast

pace on a heading that will take it out to sea beyond Haifa. I can do
nothing but watch and, as the aircraft passes overhead, I pull the
Messerschmitt up vertically and peer intently through the windscreen.
The airspeed drops dramatically and, as I try to see if there are any
markings on the twin-engine machine, the Messerschmitt stalls and falls
away to one side. The earth does a half-turn under the nose and the
altimeter needle spins down to 12,000 feet. I look back at the vanishing
shufti kite. I didn't see any markings on it at all.

Kalman Turin is the adjutant at 101 Squadron and he also serves as
the Squadron Intelligence Officer. Thin and quiet, he had served in a
ground capacity with the RAF as a Palestine volunteer and had come
over from Sde Dov when 101 was formed. Efficient and well thought of,
he takes my report after I land back at Herzliya. In the Ops tent we sit in
camp chairs and Kalman scribbles on a pad but we still don't know any
more about the shufti kites then we did before.

When I come out of the tent Sid Cohen is going by in a jeep with
Croll. They stop and I ride out to the Spitfire dispersal point with them.
Sid is going on a PR flight to Gaza and as he puts on his gear I tell him
about the shufti kite episode. He laughs and goes over and looks at the
map which Croll seems eternally to have in his hand. A Messerschmitt is
taking off and we can't hear anything for a minute. Sid wipes his mouth
with his forearm. When he gets up on the wing of the Spitfire, Croll
extends a revolver in a fabric holster toward him. He tells Croll he
doesn't want it. He says they are too bulky to wear in the cockpit and that
they are dangerous to be carrying if you are captured. Croll agrees but
says it is an order from Headquarters that the reconnaissance pilots must
wear a sidearm. Sid still doesn't want it. Croll looks at the ground beside
the wing for a moment. He says it's not necessarily for use against the
enemy. He says it's for Sid to use on himself if he is captured by
irregulars. The statement amuses Sid. He takes the gun and straps it on
and climbs into the cockpit.

With the arrival of September the status along the fronts remained
unchanged and the UN progress in the mediations seemed hopelessly
bogged down. At Herzliya most of the information comes to us by rumor
or from the *Palestine Post* or by English-language radio broadcasts from
Tel Aviv or Beirut or Cairo. When anything is reported in Hebrew or
Arab we get Ezer or Sandy Jacobs to translate it. The waiting continues
and the Messerschmitts remain a paradox. The accidents haven't taken
any lives yet but when everyone gathered in the evening outside the
porch at Kafr Shmaryahu and the talk came around to the machines as it
always did, the unspoken thought in everyone's mind was who would be
the first permanent victim.

At the beginning of the new month an order comes down requiring
the pilots to serve a night as Duty Officer as the rotation dictated. By the
end of the first week I have the assignment and when I arrive at the

Command hut it is almost dark and the light is on in the office. Kalman is inside with sergeant of the guard Avrom Levi, whose regular Squadron assignment is as an armorer on Messerschmitt 120. Levi smiles and tips a finger to his frayed beret when I come into the room. Kalman is leaving and I go over to Moddy's desk and put the gun belt on. In the holster is a British Webley .38 caliber pistol. I look at Levi. A Palestinian Jew, he is husky and has a black moustache, and eyelids that perpetually droop so that he appears constantly unconcerned. He was with Irgun at one time and his early training with the Jewish Brigade is evident in his speech and bearing. We walk outside to where the duty jeep is parked and we can see Miriam at the switchboard behind the doorless entrance of the Communications shack. Levi says something to her in Hebrew. We get in the jeep and Levi moves his pistol holster around so that it rests on his lap when he is driving. The guards at the planes are inspected every two hours throughout the night. Levi turns on the jeep lights and we make the first tour. From the passenger seat I look into the darkness ahead and I can barely distinguish the dispersal areas out on the field. We drive down past the grove revetments and the mechanic guard is standing near the last one on the line. His rifle is propped against an oil drum. Levi stops and they speak in Hebrew for a moment, then both the guard and Levi light cigarettes and we start off again. We go out around the western perimeter and the hooded headlights of the jeep faintly pick out the form of a Messerschmitt. We pull to a stop beside the camouflage net connectors. The sentry comes around from behind the aircraft and hails us. Levi says something and then pushes the vehicle into gear and we go back to the administration section.

The administration area is deserted except for those on duty and the only lights are the dim lamps inside the Communications and Command huts. These all-night duty sessions soon acquire the stigma of becoming boring as the hours wear on and, even though we have the company of the telephone girls, the lack of excitement, along with the necessity of remaining awake, makes the morning seem far away. Avrom Levi had a remedy for all this. He goes across to the mess hall and gets an empty fruit jar from behind the kitchen and we drive into Herzliya and get it filled with cognac at a cafe. The place is crowded with soldiers and girls and the old man at the counter fills the jar from a barrel in the back. We drink a glass of the cognac at the counter before we leave. On the road into camp the cognac sloshes around in the jar and we take another drink and it spills on the front of our shirts.

The inspection rounds become increasingly unmilitary. Levi stands up behind the steering wheel of the jeep and shouts 'shalom' as we speed by the sentry posts. On the ten o'clock tour, Levi cuts away at the east boundary and drives into the hillside fields on the upper edge of Kafr Shmaryahu, where the land girls are employed in night irrigation. We park on an incline and Levi jokes with the girls and they laugh and throw

dirt clods at us. When we leave we go through the sprinklers and over
the pipes and when we get back down to the strip, Levi plows into the
dirt furrow without seeing it. The jeep is flung violently upward and Levi
is catapulted out of the driver's seat and disappears into the darkness.
The jeep continues on for another 20 yards, barely missing one of the
empty fuel drum markers that are spaced along the furrow, and then it
swerves to the right and jerks to a stop, the motor choking into silence.
With the initial impact I had grabbed the side of the windshield frame
and hung on as the suddenly driverless vehicle skidded along on its own
course. After the jeep stops, I look around for Levi and he comes running
up and jumps back into the seat and starts the motor again without a
word. We surge forward and bounce across the end of the strip. Levi is
plastered with dirt and his shirt is torn and his knees are bleeding below
the cuff of his tropical shorts. His gun holster is around on the back of
his belt. He laughs.

When we get to the Command hut and park the jeep, Miriam comes
out of Communications and looks at us. We go inside the hut and Levi
gets the fruit jar from the floor behind the desk. The quart container is
almost empty. We take another drink and then Miriam runs in from next
door and says we have to go to Tel Aviv. Someone had telephoned from
a bistro in town and said one of the groundcrew from 101 Squadron was
causing a lot of trouble in the cafe and we better come in and pick him
up before the MPs did. Levi finishes the contents of the jar and puts it
down. He points to Moddy's desk where the Duty Officer's arm band is
lying. I hadn't worn it all evening but now I go over and put it on. It is
black with two Hebrew letters in red and I put it on upside down. Levi
is on his way out to the jeep and, at the doorway, he turns around and
goes back and gets the fruit jar. He says we'll get some more cognac in
Tel Aviv.

We travel the road to Tel Aviv at high speed and when we arrive at the
suburbs we encounter a number of other vehicles. Levi turns the jeep in
and out between them and at one corner we go over a curb and then jolt
back out onto the pavement. We hear shouts coming from the lorry
behind us. The bistro is on a side street near Ben Yehuda and when we
get there we can't find a place to park so Levi parks the jeep on the
sidewalk. There is a big crowd and we get out of the jeep and walk past
the outside tables and into the packed interior of the bistro. Levi has the
fruit jar in his hand. We go up to the bar and he requests that the jar be
filled with cognac. The proprietor has his shirt sleeves rolled up above
the elbow and he takes the fruit jar and looks without comment at the
upside-down armband and the stained clothes and bloody knees. He
points to a table near the entrance. The only one in the bistro who isn't
making any noise is the one he is pointing at. It is Reuben, an engine
mechanic on Messerschmitt 115. He has had too much to drink and he
rests his head on the table while those with him sing and laugh. The

proprietor suggests we take Reuben with us while he's quiet. Levi orders two cognacs at the bar and pays the proprietor and we drink and watch the tables. Two soldiers come up beside us and insist that we have a drink with them. They are drunk also. Both of them have red faces and they are Gentiles and, as soon as they speak, we know they are British. A piano starts playing at the far end of the room. The soldiers say they are Irish. They were with a tank regiment in the British Army and they deserted with an armored car and are now with a battalion of the Alexandroni Brigade at Latrun. They buy us a drink and begin to sing. Levi finishes the drink in one swallow and sings with them. The piano stops and we walk over to the table and Levi tells Reuben it's time to go. The others help Reuben to his feet. We get him outside and into the back seat of the jeep and then Levi places the fruit jar carefully on the floor of the front seat. The Irish soldiers follow us out, carrying their drinks. When we bump onto the street in the jeep they are singing again and the refrain slowly fades away behind us – 'Whether on the gallows high or on the battle fields we die; no matter, if for Erin fair we fall'.

The day dawns hot and the fruit jar is empty. Our eyes are red as we sit in the hut and watch the flies land on the walls. There are people moving outside and the sound of the Messerschmitt engines running up is loud on the perimeter. Sergeant of the guard Avrom Levi yawns and gets up from a chair in the corner and tips a finger to his beret. The night is over.

By the second week in September the modified Messerschmitts had become active on the PR sorties. On a day when there is a stiff breeze and small white clouds drift against a dazzling blue sky, the pilots gather before the map which is spread on the flat plywood table in the Ops tent. Three reconnaissance missions are planned simultaneously. I get a parachute from the rear of the tent and go over and look at the map. The others are already studying it and Croll shows me the course on the Jerusalem run. He taps the section where the Trans-Jordan lines cut the city in half and says to make the run in the Spitfire at 12,000 feet. The two Messerschmitt pilots collect their flying gear from a wooden rack beside the table. Leon Frankel is assigned the mission to Jericho in Trans-Jordan and Sandy is taking the low-level flight among the hills to Nablus in the middle of the salient. Sid Cohen comes in through the tent flap and there is a lot of joking about Nablus because of the large numbers of Arab homosexuals reputed to reside there. Sid tells Sandy to avoid a forced-landing at any costs and everyone laughs except Sandy. Sid drives us around to the revetments in the jeep and he says he got a lot of anti-aircraft fire on the morning mission to Rafah at the Sinai border. I jump off the jeep when we get to the Spitfire and the crew sergeant, Shimon, is standing by the four-bladed propeller. He motions that the aircraft is ready to go. The machine is painted the same colors as the Messerschmitts and it is assigned the number 130. When I get into the cockpit the pistol that Croll gave me at the Ops tent is jammed under the parachute straps. I extricate it and put it to the side of the seat.

I pass over the large Arab town of Ramallah and approach Jerusalem from the north and the city is etched beneath the wings in intricate detail. The mission is entirely peaceful and I see Frankel's Messerschmitt, tiny to the east, heading across the Jordan for Jericho. I contemplate the magnitude of the history below and I am unable to reconcile the past with now. I think of our discussions at Kafr Shmaryahu and all of us here in the Holy Land fighting a war so the Jews can have a homeland for the first time in 2,000 years. We never talk about religion. I look below again. All I can see are the military targets.

A Flight and the Spitfire Brigade are preparing to leave quarters for the airfield one morning and some of the off-duty pilots are sitting in the chairs under the acacia tree. A moderate wind is blowing and the leaves and the flanks of the hedges are fluttering with it. Everyone around the tree is talking. They are talking about who is going to shoot Bill Pomerantz's dog. The pudgy Pomerantz, who is from Miami, is dressed in a colorful sport shirt and knee-length shorts and he is sitting on one of the beach chairs, holding a small dog on his lap. The dog has been ill for two days and now, plainly, it is dying. Bubbles of foam come from the nostrils as it looks up glassy-eyed at Pomerantz. Everyone agrees that is should be put out of its misery but Bill won't do it and no one else will volunteer.

Bill brushes flies away from the dog's mouth and looks from face to face around the circle of those beneath the tree. He skips past Sandy because Sandy doesn't like the animal and impudently refers to it as a wog dog. Bill's expression is almost comically sad and his gaze comes around to Giddy. Giddy shakes his head and says it's Bill's dog and that he should shoot it. Bill shakes his head and speaks to Red Finkel in Yiddish. Red declines in English. The dog tries to move and its legs twitch and it kicks Bill in the crotch. There is laughter but then everyone is silent and there is only the sound of the wind in the leaves. Chris Magee comes out of a room behind the porch. He has the red handkerchief around his head and an automatic pistol is in the belt of his flight suit. Bill gets up from the chair and carries the dog over to where Magee is standing near the porch. No one says anything and we can see Bill gesturing and finally Magee nods and they walk around the corner of the building to the maize field. In a moment Bill comes back without the dog and stops near the tent and then we hear a noise like a tree branch breaking and Magee reappears with the gun still in his hand. He motions over his shoulder with his thumb and Bill goes slowly out to the field again.

The photographic-reconnaissance missions in mid-September began to encounter increasing anti-aircraft resistance and in some cases the hostile barrages were disconcertingly accurate. Both Maury Mann and

Arni Ruch received shell splinters through the tails of 130 and Sid Cohen was followed out to sea by some of the bursts at Gaza.

The Egyptian-held coastal town of Majdal is on the main supply route to the enemy forces which are camped at Isdud and, because of its strategic position, it was considered worthy of frequent aerial observation by Military Intelligence. It now lies passive and white next to the deep blue of the sea as I turn on to the final camera run. It is a half hour past midday and at 10,000 feet the eight miles from Majdal north to Isdud seem no distance at all. I look down through the sundrenched air and line the Spitfire along the sliver of connecting road and switch on the camera.

Five darkly-blooming flowers appear magically off the port wingtip. Although they are at the same altitude, the shell bursts are not alarmingly close but their mere presence is unnerving and I try to concentrate on keeping the nose of the aircraft on a straight course. More anti-aircraft bursts begin to unfold ahead and then again, off the left wing, another pattern of shells arrives and I can see the flash of the explosion in the center of the last one that came up. Beneath the drifting smoke puffs a trail of Bofors tracers arches skyward and they are bright as they curve up with deadly grace against the dark background of the sea. I have an intense impulse to maneuver the aircraft evasively but I restrain the urge and finish the run. The film ends and I open the throttle and, a thousand feet below, I see the dispersing layer of grey haze left by the lighter pom-pom shells. In three minutes I am over Israeli territory.

From the open cockpit of the Spitfire the view is unrestricted but the wind rushes over the top of the windscreen with force. On the right side of the cowling two of the engine panel fastenings have sprung loose, and the air is beginning to get under the section in a dangerous manner. I reduce speed but the panel has a good chance of tearing away and when I am opposite Tel Aviv I spiral the machine down from the seaward side and land on the runway that parallels the shore at Sde Dov. There is a 90 degree crosswind coming in along the beach but I manage to drop down before the danger marker and, at the dirt near the end of the strip, I turn and taxi back toward the Operations shack.

Some of the groundcrew around the utility planes come over when I shut the engine off on the sunbaked southern border of the field and they are smiling because they don't see the fighters down here. The strips are too short for the Messerschmitts. I leave the parachute and helmet on the seat and get out on the wing. The cowling metal is hot when I reach forward and snap the panel buttons back into place with a five-mil piece. The groundcrew are still smiling and inspecting the Spitfire and I get down from the wing and walk over to the Ops shack.

I don't see Mischa Keren, but Kurtz and Al Schwimmer are standing out in front of the building. They are laughing and Schwimmer holds out his hand. I am glad to see him and Schwimmer says they just came in from Ramat David in the Lockheed Lodestar which is sitting out on the grass apron. He says he now has Israeli citizenship and he tells a funny story about his hurried departure from the States. He has on sweaty khakis and he puts his hands in his pockets and laughs. Some of the Sde Dov pilots have joined us and while we are talking one of the Norseman reconnaissance planes taxies by and blows sand over everyone. Schwimmer and Kurtz walk back to the Spitfire with me and I tell them about the mission to Majdal. Kurtz whistles when I mention the volume of the anti-aircraft fire and Schwimmer just keeps smiling. They say they are going into Tel Aviv and when I get into the cockpit Schwimmer waves and they go back over to Operations. The crosswind is stronger when I take off for Herzliya.

If anyone played a singularly key part in the inauguration of the Air Force in the new Israel of 1948, it was the smiling Al Schwimmer. His ingenuity and energy were behind almost every aircraft that was ferried from the States in the first months. The transports, the bombers and, because of the transports, the fighters. Schwimmer not only procured the aircraft, he gathered many of the volunteers who served during that year and he put everything he had on the line. Because of the laws of the times he eventually had to lose everything privately but, when it mattered the most, he won his personal war for Israel.

The summer was coming to an end and incident piled upon incident. On one of the September days Bernadotte is assassinated at Jerusalem. We hear the news on the radio at Falk's when we return from afternoon duty. The Jews had assassinated him and everyone knew right away that it was the extremist faction. Stern Gang was the most frequently mentioned name during the evening. Haganah deplored the act and at Kafr Shmaryahu that night we wonder about the motivation behind this violent termination of the UN Mediator. Perhaps the rumors we had heard about concessions were true but, still, the assassination was totally unexpected and the ramifications were unlimited. Bernadotte had been in the open rear seat of his official car and was proceeding to a scheduled conference when the car was stopped by several vehicles in the Jewish section. Three people, one of whom was a girl, ran over to where the Mediator was sitting and someone placed a Sten gun automatic on Bernadotte's chest and pulled the trigger. One news reporter who was witness to the event seemed fascinated by the fact that the ribbons on Bernadotte's uniform were shredded by the blast and bits of them floated off on the breeze. At Kafr Shmaryahu everyone talks about the assassination and someone says that the Arabs will have a lot of fuel for their propaganda machine tomorrow.

B Flight has the afternoon duty and Giddy is due out on a patrol. I walk with him to the revetment of Messerschmitt 119. The armorer has been checking one of the cannon ammunition drums on the machine and he goes from the cannon to the side plate on the fuselage and looks at the feeder belt on the port machine-gun. He nods and steps down from the wing. Giddy gets ready and 30 yards up the line Cyril Horowitz starts the engine on 117 and pulls away from the camouflage net. Lichtman climbs into the cockpit of 119 and a Belgian mechanic prepares to turn the inertia crank. The one everyone calls 'The Belgian' is short and wide and is the only crewman in the Squadron who is strong enough to work the handle alone. Coming from five years in a German forced labor camp, his face is prematurely old and now it shows strain as he pulls down on the crank. The muscles of his naked upper torso expand. Above the whining of the inertia we can hear Cyril open the throttle to take off. We can't see him because the corner of the revetment obstructs the view of the southern end of the strip, but as soon as the engine sound reaches a certain pitch there is the rending report of an impact and the engine becomes abruptly silent. The Belgian stops winding and Giddy jumps from the cockpit and everyone runs out in front of the revetment. Cyril has taken off into a jeep.

Some of the other pilots and groundcrew are already there when we get across the field to where the Messerschmitt is merged with a maintenance vehicle. What had occurred is obvious. Cyril had fallen victim to the torque and had allowed the aircraft to swing off at a quarter angle. It had hit the jeep on a frontal course at the west perimeter. The two mechanics in the jeep had leapt out when they saw the Messerschmitt bearing down on them and now they are standing nervously behind the wreckage. The plane and the vehicle had traveled along together after the collision and the undercarriage of the Messerschmitt had folded. The debris is way off the strip and the earth is plowed up for 50 yards. Cyril is over at the ambulance. He has a cut across the top of his nose and blood has run down onto his handlebar moustache. He is dazed and wants to know what happened. Under the circumstances no one finds it necessary to tell him. The ambulance is marked with a red Star of David and Cyril is helped into the back. They leave for the infirmary at the far side of the mess hall. I look over at the Messerschmitt. The long-suffering Harry Axelrod is standing near the tilted wing and staring without emotion at the smashed propeller spinner.

During September the Squadron acquired two additional aircraft. They are in totally different categories because one is a P-51 Mustang fighter and the other is a little Seabee amphibian. The story behind the P-51 was interesting in the fact that it had arrived in Israel in a crate marked as farm implements, and had actually cleared US Customs as such. It had eventually made its way into Haifa harbor aboard a run-down Greek freighter and after being transferred to the docks it was immediately sent down to Herzliya, where it was re-assembled. When it was airworthy again, Giddy, who was partial to P-51s to the point of fanaticism, was designated to test it. It flew well on its first flight and the only problem deterring it from full operational status at the time was a complete absence of spare parts. Notwithstanding this problem, he managed to fly the aircraft frequently during the month.

The Seabee became, almost immediately, the plaything of Ezer. Although Moddy and a few of the others flew the ugly little underpowered craft occasionally, Ezer flew it whenever he wasn't engaged in operations and he was constantly luring others to take a ride in it. It was to provide one of those tales that became more exaggerated with time. When the Squadron had been relieved one afternoon, Ezer started up the Seabee and began to look around for passengers. By the time the engine was warmed up he had convinced Red Finkel, Maury Mann and Bill Pomerantz to accompany him on a local flight. They all climbed into the four-place machine and when the Seabee took off it barely cleared the hill at Kafr Shmaryahu, and then disappeared from view behind the slope to the north-west. Those who were watching stared at the empty sky and we didn't know what happened until Ezer brought the plane back an hour later.

They had gone down to buzz the beach. The Communications girls were there waving from the sand. Ezer decided to land in the water behind the breakers. Everything went well until they got on the surface of the sea. One of the wing floats was damaged when they hit a large swell and the pull of the surf started to carry the small plane toward the shore. Ezer applied the rudder until they were headed into the wind and opened the throttle to take off. With the shortage of power in the engine, and with the heavy-bodied Maury and Bill in the rear seats, the amphibian hummed along over the waves but refused to lift into the air. Ezer closed the throttle. He thought their dilemma was extremely funny and rested his head on the control column and shook with laughter. Next to him Red looked out the side window and his only reaction was a quiet smile. The others laughed but neither was really amused because they suspected what the ultimate solution to the problem was going to be. Ezer tried three more runs but they remained steadfastly on the water. Someone was going to have to get out. Red couldn't swim and both Maury and Bill were poor swimmers so they flipped a coin. Maury lost. He didn't like it and he threw the ten-mil piece disgustedly out of the window. He began to take off his shoes. Ezer maneuvered the Seabee parallel to the shore line but he had to stay at least 200 yards out. Maury conceded that he was going to get wet so he took off his shirt and trousers as well. The amphibian was rising and dropping on the swells and he waited until they were on the crest of one and plunged out. He ripped the seat off his underwear on the door handle as he left.

At the base camp the Seabee swings around near the Ops tent and Ezer, Red and Bill get out. They say it still took a two-mile run to get airborne after Maury departed. Everybody is laughing. They send a jeep down to the beach to pick up the swimmer. The sun has set and the surf is deserted and in the western glow before dark they can see the solitary figure lying on his back in the sand with his hands behind his head, gazing upward at the descending night.

Soon the high winds of the autumn equinox begin blowing. They come in from the east and on some days the aircraft have to be tied down and we spend our time in the tents. There is a moaning sound overhead and the flying sand punishes the canvas outside. During lulls, when there is only a fierce breeze, we are in the air again. The unforgiving Messerschmitts demand more skill than ever.

CHAPTER VII

THE INTERLUDE ACTIONS

It is a morning that is hardly suitable for flying the Desert Hawks but I taxi to the south perimeter and, when I turn upfield, the wind is so strong that I continue around in a complete circle. When I finally line up with the strip I can see that a dust layer has ascended to 3,000 feet above Kafr Shmaryahu. I am ready to open the throttle when I see Giddy running toward me from the Ops tent. I let the engine idle. It is back firing as Giddy comes around behind the port aileron and gets up on the step panel next to the cockpit. The wind tugs furiously at his clothes. I open the canopy. Giddy is shouting but I still have to remove the helmet to hear what he is saying. He bends his head forward into the cockpit and says that the red Rapide has been reported over Safad again. Giddy doesn't have to explain what he means. For a week we have known that a red Rapide has been periodically violating Israeli airspace and it is always in the same area of the Galil. I nod and close the canopy.

When I get in the air it is bumpy and I climb north along the edge of the salient. I can see where the Alexandroni Brigade has positions along the border and at 6,000 feet I pass Kafr Yona which had been shelled in the May fighting. Beyond, the Natanya auxiliary base lies windswept in the sun. At 12,000 feet I am above Nazareth and the wind keeps blowing me westward. I correct for the drift and turn toward the Galil. For a half hour I circle the vicinity of Safad but I don't see anything so I climb higher and return to the Israel corridor between the salient and the sea to look for shufti kites.

Two days later Giddy encountered the red Rapide. He was making a last turn above Safad before returning to Herzliya. The area below was not unfamiliar to him because he had been coming to the same place for the past three days. As he began the final sweep he saw the two-winged transport plane cutting across the airspace east of Safad and some five miles behind the Israeli front-line outposts. The foreign aircraft was undeniably red in color and at 5,000 feet it was slightly below the Messerschmitt. The Rapide apparently didn't see the Israeli aircraft and it continued south, halfway between Safad and the Syrian border and heading toward Lake Tiberius. Giddy immediately rolled downward and passed beyond the slower moving machine and took a position between it and the settlement of Mishmar Ha'Yarden, which was the Jewish town directly on the frontier. It can be stated early of this incident that Giddy employed proper procedure in accordance with an Air Command order, in the attempt to persuade the unidentified aircraft to land before more extreme measures were applied. The transport ignored the presence of the fighter momentarily and then it changed direction suddenly and headed east. It passed beneath Giddy, who had to maneuver sharply to stay to the port quarter. The Rapide proceeded on the revised course toward the sanctuary of the Arab lines beyond the Jordan River. Giddy edged in toward the other craft and, lowering the undercarriage on the Messerschmitt, he signaled to the pilot of the Rapide that he wished him to land in Israeli territory. Giddy had the intention at this point of escorting the transport down to the base at Ramat David. The Rapide pilot was apparently not similarly inclined and the aircraft again cut under the Messerschmitt.

By now Giddy was becoming angry because he was having difficulty handling the fighter at the slower speed, and he could clearly see that they were nearing the Syrian border. He moved in close again and he observed Arabic script on the fuselage of the red Rapide and what he termed 'bearded, turbaned faces gawking from the cabin windows'. He had to extend the flaps partially to avoid overshooting the other plane and he motioned toward the ground again. The Rapide drifted outward and this time Giddy fired a burst from his machine-guns across the flight path of the disobedient aircraft. The glowing tracer bullets left a brief trail and succeeded in forcing the transport into a dive toward the river.

There wasn't any more time left. The red Rapide would be clear in 30 seconds. The nose of the Messerschmitt followed the descending craft. They are down to 2,000 feet and the sections of the fields near the river are below them. The form of the transport moves into the gunsight of the Messerschmitt, looming nearer as the higher speed of the fighter quickly closes the distance between the two aircraft. Giddy fires directly at the red Rapide. The cannons pump out three rounds and then they jam and the bright color keeps turning away in front of him. He fires the machine-guns and the rivet-like tracers fly outward again. The red Rapide goes down.

At Herzliya we gather around the returning Messerschmitt and its appearance seems properly sinister. We were waiting for it because the base tower had called Operations and reported the interception of the red Rapide. Giddy is excited and he stands beside the fuselage and his voice is high-pitched when be talks. Everyone is listening to him and Moddy and Ezer are smiling. The Rapide had gone into a spiral after the burst of machine-gun fire had smashed into the starboard engine and set the fuel tank alight. The fabric on the machine became quickly enveloped in flames but the height and momentum of the falling aircraft carried it across the river where it struck the ground near some Iraqi positions. This fact was going to result in charges being hurled but for now Giddy takes a drink from a canteen and says no one in the Rapide could have survived the crash.

The day passes. Intelligence at the Yarkon listens for reaction from Arab sources and foreign news reports are monitored but as the afternoon progresses there is no mention of the incident. We still don't know the identity of the red Rapide. The day ends and we go back to Kafr Shmaryahu and after a meal we go down to the roadhouse. Nothing is discussed except the affair of the morning and at the roadhouse we drink and wait for the nine o'clock English-language news relayed from Beirut. The wireless-radio behind the bar is sending forth the exotic sound of Arabic music which suddenly subsides when the news broadcast is presented. The first item is about the downed transport.

Neither Giddy nor anyone else was prepared for the version that now unfolded over the air waves. Everyone unconsciously leans forward at the tables as the English voice recites. The Arabs are charging Israel with an atrocity. They are claiming that an unarmed civilian transport plane which was en route from Beirut to Amman was intercepted over Syrian territory and shot down without warning by an Israeli fighter. There are murmurs at the tables and the voice on the radio continues. It says that the British pilot of the Arab Airways' Rapide survived the crash with minor injuries as did two others who were aboard. Another four passengers were killed, including two well known British foreign correspondents* and two minor Arab potentates. Everyone looks at Giddy. He is incredulous. He gets up from the table and says he doesn't understand how anyone could have survived the crash. It is apparent that the Arabs are coming out with a story that is the opposite to the Israeli report of the incident. It doesn't surprise anyone and no one believes it. Sid Cohen laughs and says that's what they're expected to say. More details are given by the radio commentator. The pilot of the Rapide claims that everyone on board would have survived but that the four who were killed jumped out of the plane before it got to the ground. Giddy stares at the floor and shakes his head from side to side. The furore was stemming from the Arab assertion that the Messerschmitt came into Arab airspace and from the fact that two allegedly neutral British newspapermen were killed. The quiet Hebrew accent of Moddy's voice is heard and he comes over and puts his hand on Giddy's shoulder. He tells him not to worry. He says the Arabs are making propaganda. The news broadcast has moved to another subject and someone turns it off and the room is suddenly filled with loud talk. Ezer can be heard above

---

* The two British correspondents were John Nixon of the BBC and David Woodford of *The Daily Telegraph*.

the others. He says that the British correspondents were definitely not neutral. They were on the Stern Gang 'list'.

Reactions to the red Rapide incident hadn't died away when the shufti kite episode occurred and this mission was to retain a certain aura of mystery. Wayne Peake [a newly arrived American volunteer] in this instance was on patrol without oxygen at the remarkable height of 21,000 feet. He somehow managed to proceed on the flight at this altitude without passing out and, when he was above Cape Carmel with the sun directly overhead, he saw a Mosquito approaching at high speed. The shufti kite was 2,000 feet below and Peake had to react quickly. He completed a maneuver which brought the Messerschmitt [in fact Peake was flying the newly acquired P-51, *not* a Messerschmitt] just about behind the Mosquito but at a considerable range. He shoved the throttle all the way forward. The intruder aircraft reacted also and Peake could see the twin streaks of dark mist coming from its exhausts, suggesting that maximum power had been applied. A chase began that coursed across Haifa and over the harbor and out to sea. Peake soon realised that the Messerschmitt [*sic*] was not gaining on the shufti kite and that he was in danger of dropping out of range entirely.

To follow the Air Command procedure with this unidentified aircraft would be preposterous and Peake adjusted the gunsight setting and peered through the reflector. The Mosquito had no visible markings and was of a light color on the upper surfaces. As it became framed in the sight at a three-quarter angle, Peake fired an extreme deflection burst. It gave no evidence of having found its mark and one of the cannons jammed, causing the Messerschmitt [*sic*] to swerve to the left. Peake cursed and pulled farther to port of the other machine. He tried another deflection shot with the one cannon and both machine-guns. The tracers appeared to be on a strange trajectory and were curving away from the Mosquito. Peake put pressure on the starboard rudder control. Suddenly the port engine cowl of the leading aircraft revealed the tell-tale flashes of bullet strikes and a thin stream of pale smoke erupted from the exhausts. It continued on a level plane for a few seconds and then it threw its left propeller and the cowling disintegrated and bits of metal trailed behind like so many silver butterflies. It then went into a steep, rolling dive which Peake had difficulty imitating. Down below the shufti kite began to break up, continuing its uncontrolled dive until it plunged into the sea 12 miles off the Ladder of Tyre in Lebanese waters.

Silence from the other side not only greeted this action, it persisted. Intelligence interrogated Peake and as much information as possible was obtained. No recognizable insignia had been observed on the other aircraft. No parachutes were seen ejecting from the falling Mosquito but the glare from both sun and sea were strong and there could have been parachutes. No return fire had been noticed. For obvious reasons no one wanted to claim ownership of the shufti kite and so there was silence.

There were some ground witnesses in Acre who saw the encounter from afar but they were unable to supply pertinent details. Whispers that the victim was British were barely audible for the rest of the month*.

After all the agonizing, oxygenless patrols, the Squadron was elated that a shufti kite had finally been brought down but this novelty also passed as October neared. More and more armed clashes were developing on the fronts in spite of the ceasefire. The UN peacekeeping force was inadequate and unrealistic and the negotiations continued to be unproductive. Guarded reaction had hailed the arrival of the new UN Mediator, Dr Ralph Bunche, who had replaced the late Count Bernadotte at the end of September, but Bunche's task of arranging a peace acceptable to all the combatants appeared, at best, monumental. The situation was volatile.

The month had brought other developments in 101 Squadron. Chris Magee returned to the States and Cyril Horowitz was taken off flying duty and assigned to a job with Headquarters fighter operations at the Yarkon. A strong rumor was circulating that the Spitfire purchase had been concluded in Czechoslovakia – and I had to crash-land one of the Messerschmitts.

The wind had been blowing hard during the previous night but that morning it was comparatively calm and we got the patrols off. Sid Antin gives me a ride in the jeep and I get out at the dispersal area of Messerschmitt 121. It is another shufti kite mission. At 14,000 feet the supercharger cuts in and I feel the added power surge in the engine and the manifold pressure increases. I fly far to the north. Passing above Acre I proceed over Nihariya and the sky is deserted when, after an hour, I turn toward the east. Tiberius hovers ahead and I lose track of time in the high solitude. I have a headache from the altitude, and from the drinking at Kafr Shmaryahu the previous night, and when I bank southward again I remember to check the fuel reading. The litre content is low. I look at the clock on the instrument panel. It is past eleven and I have been out for over an hour and a half. I turn for Herzliya.

On the downwind leg at the base strip the red warning light is indicating ten minutes of fuel left. Plenty of time. I call the tower and turn onto the base segment and lower the undercarriage. I can feel the shudder as it extends and I am pulling on the flap wheel when I see that the undercarriage light is still red. I close the throttle and the warning horn sounds ominously. I check the gear indicator on the instrument panel. It shows the starboard leg locked in the down position and the port leg stuck at the half-extended mark. I return the handle to 'up'. Nothing happens. I put it down again. Nothing. Hydraulic failure. I look beneath and I am over the groves and coming into the final approach.

---

* Wayne Peake had in fact shot down an RAF Mosquito PR34 of 13 Squadron flying from Fayid in the Canal Zone, in which Flg Off Eric Reynolds and Nav 2 Angus Love were killed.

The strip is directly ahead and I open the throttle and go around. I pass low over Herzliya and I resort to flinging the aircraft from side to side in the hope of forcing the errant leg to lock down. When this fails I try the dangerous centrifugal force remedy and execute a tight vertical turn above the center of town.

In the streets below everyone is looking skyward. This maneuver is also met with negative results and I start to regain altitude when the power cuts off and the propeller slows to windmill speed. The fuel has run out. I switch on the emergency fuel pump and the engine coughs to life again but it is clear that time has run out. The emergency system might provide another minute of flying but it is doubtful that I can obtain the proper height to use my parachute, so the decision becomes fundamentally simple. I must get into the strip and land with one undercarriage leg down and one not down. My mind races and yet I seem to be unreasonably calm and my consciousness had been spared apprehension because everything has happened too quickly. The realization of what could lie ahead is mercifully prohibited from entering my thoughts. I turn onto the approach again and the strip is still waiting. I see the ambulance and the fire truck crossing the boundary. The jeeps are trailing them to the eastern perimeter. On the road between the mess hall and the Ops tent a crowd has gathered and many of the groundcrew are standing in front of the revetments on the south path. The Messerschmitt is descending fast and the voice from the tower has ceased calling. There is silence in the earphones of the helmet. I try to imagine that I am performing a normal landing. The trees at the end of the grove rush past and the strip rises closer. The aircraft drops onto the dusty surface.

When the Messerschmitt touches the ground it rolls for a distance on the extended wheel and then the opposite wing drops and contacts the earth. Things take place in rapid sequence. The most fortunate event in the series is the collapsing of the down gear leg which immediately causes the machine to flop onto its belly. Simultaneously with this occurrence, the propeller shatters into flying shards of wood and chunks of dirt and parts of the plane's underside begins to follow in the wake of the still fast-moving and potentially lethal aircraft.

I sit in the cockpit and grip the now useless control stick and I have no thoughts at all. It is like waiting for a story to end. The aircraft itself will write the final paragraph. It is on its own and I have nothing more to do with its progress or direction. I am merely a passenger now and its whim will dictate how the chapter will close.

With the initial impact I am jarred forward but the harness holds taut and now I travel oddly near the ground, down the middle of the strip. I look through the center of the windscreen but I concentrate on nothing. Slowly the machine veers to the right and its speed still seems exceptionally high. Its change of course puts it on a direct line with the fire truck and all at once this mandatory acquiescence to the aircraft's preferences injects me with an overwhelming feeling of helplessness. The marker drums on the east boundary race up and suddenly the fire truck becomes an insurmountable obstacle. All motion becomes like the stop-action frames of a camera. The two occupants of the vehicle sit tensely on the high, old-fashioned seat above the red-painted hood and in the first frame we stare at one another in disbelief. The next frame shows two figures leaping wildly through the air. The nose of the Messerschmitt plows into the dirt furrow and the machine is propelled upward onto its spinner where it hangs, tail straight up, for several suspenseful seconds. Then it falls, with a certain curious dignity, back onto its belly. It has stopped five feet away from the fire truck.

Moddy, Ezer, Sid Cohen and Harry Axelrod are the first ones to reach the side of the cockpit. I open the canopy and the dust is stifling and when I get out it seems strange to be able to step directly onto the ground.

* * * * *

A week before September ended Moddy, Arni and Sid Cohen are summoned to the Yarkon and advised that they will be travelling to Czechoslovakia. The Spitfires had been purchased. Five of the ex-RAF machines at Budejovice had been procured and there were indications that even more were being sought from the Czechs. Now their delivery to Israel depended in part on the 101 pilots. At Zatec, Sam Pomeranz had fitted the five aircraft with external auxiliary fuel tanks and he had devised a modification to the internal fuel system to enable the planes to have an increased range of eight hours in the air. Technically they could make the long flight to Israel non-stop. Pomeranz would also be one of the pilots on the journey. The fifth participant in this ferrying operation was the industrious Boris Senior.

Flying the much desired Spitfires from Czechoslovakia to Israel was not necessarily a difficult or dangerous project. Taken first to the Czech base at Kanovice in the extreme southern section of the country, the planes would be fuelled to capacity and begin the flight from there in the company of a C-54, which would act as a mother ship and navigate the course for the Spitfires. They would generally travel the Velveta route and pass beyond Titograd to the Adriatic and then, skirting Greek territory, make their way eastward and then south past Crete and Cyprus to Ramat David. All would go well until they were opposite the island of Rhodes.

Maury and I are to remain at Herzliya with the Spitfire Brigade. The night following the announcement of the deal, the three Europe-bound pilots are ready to leave. At Kafr Shmaryahu we see them off and there are drinks and laughter and only Moddy is serious. Boris comes in from Tel Aviv and then the four get into a jeep and head for Lydda. It is a week before we hear anything more.

Maury becomes acting CO during this period and the quiet Rudy Augarten takes over the recently appointed post of Operations Officer. Rudy has the task of supervising the Flights and, on the last evening of the month, we are sitting in Falk's garden after dinner when he comes in from the base camp with the next day's flying schedule. He also has a request from Headquarters for a special mission. They want a single-plane sortie to the Egyptian airfield at El Arish to be flown at first light in the morning. Rudy reads from a paper he is holding and everyone around the tree becomes still. It is nearly dark and the lights from inside the screen porch are casting a yellow glow on the hedges. Rudy finishes reading what is in the paper. Operations wants a low-level flight over El Arish at dawn with the PR Spitfire. The pilot is to make only one pass and he is to try to retain everything he sees while finding out how awake they are down there. No camera will be used on the mission and the fact that there is a prevailing ceasefire demands that precaution and discretion be utilized during the operation. The resurrected Egyptian Spitfire was being employed on the sortie because it has a good chance of getting in and out of the enemy area without creating undue alarm in advance. The Egyptians generally trusted Spitfires, but even a long-range glimpse of a Desert Hawk had by know become a reason for profound consternation in the Arab strongholds. Rudy repeats the last sentence of the notation – one pass over El Arish and out. Everyone knows that Maury and I are the only Spitfire pilots left in 101 and Rudy looks at me without further comment. It is a volunteer mission. Maury is in the latrine, so I tell Rudy I'll take the assignment.

The duty jeep comes round before daybreak the next morning. With Sid Cohen and Arni in Czechoslovakia, I am alone in the tent and when Rudy arrives at the entrance I am already awake. The jackals had howled persistently during the night and I had awakened and listened to them for an hour. Now it is time to go. Rudy waits while I get dressed in the dark and then we walk to the kitchen near the porch and drink some of the tea which is always left on top of the stove. We go out to the jeep and the garden shrubs are obscure when we pass through. We get in the jeep and take the rutted road down to the base camp. We are both sleepy and we don't talk. When we arrive at the Spitfire dispersal, the groundcrew is preparing to run the engine up. In the east a streak of light is now visible. Shimon is in the cockpit and in a few moments he throttles the engine back and the half-light permits one to see the blue flame that flickers hypnotically from the exhaust stacks. Shimon gets out of the cockpit and I take the parachute from the edge of the wing and climb up and get in. After I fasten the safety belt Rudy steps up beside the windscreen. He has to speak above the idling engine and he wants to know if I will need illumination from the lights of the jeep at the north end of the strip to orient the aircraft on the take-off. I pull the helmet on and look over my shoulder. The sky is growing paler by the minute. I shake my head. Rudy gets down and walks back to the jeep and I ease the throttle forward and turn upfield.

The day is fast arriving when I pass over Petah Tiqva. I haven't risen higher than 2,000 feet and after I turn down the coast beyond Jaffa I drop close above the waves of the sea. I stay three miles out and parallel the contours of the shore line. A ship which I assume to be an Israeli corvette is making its way southward off Jaffa. I watch it for a moment and then it falls behind and I dismiss it and begin to think of other things. I wonder about the ground defenses at El Arish and I wonder how alert they will be at this early hour. I don't worry about their fighters because on the missions I have thus far flown in Israel the challenges by enemy aircraft have been non-existent. The coastal flats around Majdal approach and recede and Gaza looms ahead. The sun is beginning to show above the ring of the eastern hills and the emerging rays cause tiny glints of light to hit the crests of the rolling swells beneath. Ashore all appears motionless and now the port wing points at Gaza.

Presently the coastline bends seaward and I pass the border of the Sinai. An odd outcropping of land juts into the sea beyond the town of El Arish and when it is in front of the Spitfire I bank sharply in and cross over the beach. The desolation of the desert spreads before the spinning propeller and the climbing sun causes shadows to creep outward in long patterns from the ridges and rocks on the arid sand dunes of the landscape. I turn north. The town and the airfield are separated by a short distance that is filled with makeshift dwellings and tents and I pull the Spitfire up to 200 feet and get a broader view. The line I am on is bringing me across the base over the south-east runway and the fact that this very machine took off from here to attack Tel Aviv in May borders on comedy.

I look alternately to the right and to the left. The fighter dispersal points, the hardstands, gun emplacements, the hangars, the REAF Dakotas scattered about and, on the eastern edge of the field under camouflage, is one of the recently acquired Fiat fighters we had heard about [it was in fact a Macchi MC205V]. I dip the starboard wing of the Spitfire but I see nothing resembling a mass buildup of aircraft. On the contrary, they seem to have moved aircraft out of the base. Below, a lorry is moving down a side road, the dust billowing upward behind it in the morning light. It is the first sign of movement I have seen. The runway ends and I pass the north border of the base and there are more tents and houses and then they fall away behind as I continue toward the sea. As I re-cross the beach I look back and a feint line of shell tracers makes an erratic pattern in the air above the base. I smile at the instrument panel. They are much too late.

The sun is higher on the return flight and it is bright in my eyes when I look at the shore. When I am nearing Majdal I see the corvette ahead, plowing through the swells on a south-westerly course. It is five miles off the coast and there is suddenly something imperceptively strange about its presence. Impulsively I turn the Spitfire outward and in a few minutes I come around behind the ship. I am low on the water and, as the vessel grows in the windscreen, I can see it rolling and pitching in the sea troughs. I am trying to identify the ensign flag which is flying at the stern when a volley of Bofors rounds rushes past the starboard wing like orange-colored tennis balls. The ship is Egyptian. I instantly turn away and, as the Spitfire's wing drops vertically near the surface, I see the flash and white smoke of a high-caliber anti-aircraft gun which is firing from the after deck. I get out of range.

The suddenness of the unfriendly salvo had surprised me and it has also instilled in me a certain amount of fear which had given way to a desire for retaliation when I was a good distance off. I release the safety of the gun control button on the stick and then I hesitate. I have thoughts of being involved in a truce violation. I remember the orders and turn for Herzliya.

It was upon landing from this mission that the sight in my right eye diminished drastically. I knew it was a recurrence of a condition caused by a war wound and the effect was usually of short duration. By the next day the vision had improved and I never mentioned anything about it.

CHAPTER VIII

DEATH OF A HERO

Three days into October we are alerted that the Spitfires from Czechoslovakia are due at Ramat David during the afternoon. An escort flight is organized and we draw cards to see who will fly it. Sandy and I get the sortie. Information from the Yarkon says the Spitfires are scheduled to cross the harbor at Haifa at four o'clock and we make our plans to intercept them and escort them the rest of the way to Ramat David.

We take two Messerschmitts and depart Herzliya at three-thirty. The Spitfires were to be flying in at 5,000 feet so we proceed toward Haifa at 6,000 feet. Near Natanya we pass the Lodestar flying up the coast and whoever is in the co-pilot's seat is smiling and waving. South of Cape Carmel we turn away from the land and go out to sea and then cut north again to the harbor. There is a haze which is aggravated by the afternoon sun but we still have fair visibility. Sandy is doggedly hanging close to my port wing and we circle an area of 20 miles of the water. We can see no other machines. We keep watching to the north and an hour passes and there is nothing else visible in the air. The circling is becoming monotonous. We are unable to contact Ramat David on the radio and we can barely hear Herzliya. They tell us to continue to search. More circling and looking toward the north. Emptiness. After another 15 minutes of the criss-cross pattern above the harbor we receive a garbled message to return to base. The wind has changed direction when we get back and we have to approach over Kafr Shmaryahu. We come into the strip high and when we get on the ground we both roll down to the grove revetments before we can stop.

Almost everyone is at the Ops tent and we hear the news. Three of the Spitfires are at Ramat David. Sid Cohen, Sam Pomeranz and Arni Ruch. They had crossed the coast north of Haifa at three-thirty but Ramat David hadn't notified Herzliya until later. Moddy and Boris had force-landed on the Greek island of Rhodes. Their reserve fuel tanks had malfunctioned and now the Spitfires were interned by the Greeks. So were Moddy and Boris.

The other three Spitfires are remaining temporarily at Ramat David to be refitted and Sid Cohen and Arni fly back to Herzliya that evening in a utility plane. When they arrive we all gather at the Command hut and they tell us about the flight down from Czechoslovakia. Sid says there were no problems until the fuel system failures west of Rhodes. He says Moddy didn't say much on the R/T at the time but that Boris was joking over the radio as they were preparing to land on the island. The other aircraft, including the C-54, had circled until the two were down on the Greek runway but they couldn't tarry and had to leave them behind. Sid and Arni are laughing although everyone feels Moddy's absence. They say that Yigael Yadin, the personable Chief of Staff of the Haganah forces, and even Ben-Gurion himself, are already negotiating to get the Greeks to release the pilots and the aircraft. Sid thinks it is an amusing coincidence that the UN Mediator, Dr Bunche, displaying understandable caution, had decided to set up his headquarters on the island of Rhodes.

On the eve of the Yom Kippur holidays the base at Herzliya is visited by a certain US Senator. He is accompanied on a tour of the airfield by Yigael Yadin and some aides and, though the ransoming of Moddy from the Greeks is on everyone's mind, nothing is said at the time. We stand by the aircraft and the visitors pass in casual review and everything is formal as usual. I look at the Desert Hawks. I couldn't have known it at that moment but I had taken my last flight in them.

The next day the holidays begin and it is a clear October evening when the party starts at Kafr Shmaryahu. Bottles are produced and there is a lot of drinking at Falk's and then we all go down to the base camp mess hall for a special meal. Tables have been arranged outside and they reach all the way over to the roadway. There is music and dancing and laughter in the air. After the food has been served at the long tables, the pilots begin to drift away into the coming night and some find their way back up to Kafr Shmaryahu. From there everyone is planning to go into Tel Aviv. Red Finkel has somehow engaged a taxi which has come over from Herzliya and he gets into the back seat with one of the new girls from camp. Four more of us crowd into the back with them and we all sit crammed together on the ride into town.

There are parties all over Tel Aviv and some of 101 are at the Park Hotel bar. It is nine o'clock and I am drinking at a table with Sid Cohen and Ezer. Dov Ben Zvi, Yacov and Lev are with us. Music is coming from somewhere near the terrace. The austere Ben Zvi* is transportation officer at Herzliya and Yacov and Lev are riggers on the Messerschmitts. Called Jake, Yacov is another who had served in the Mandate forces and he has a cynical sense of humor toward life. Lev is young but his face

---

* Dov Ben Zvi was the name adopted by British-born Baron Wiseberg, a former Royal Navy Fleet Air Arm fighter pilot who had flown with 101 Squadron early in the war.

reveals the hard lines of silently endured tragedy that one saw on many of the faces in this land. His brother had been with Irgun and was hung by the British the same week that Irgun had abducted and hung two British Army sergeants.

We drink and then Ben Zvi leaves. Sid and Ezer go up to the bar where they are joined by Giddy and Lou Lenart and some of the Yarkon people. Jake and Lev are going to a bistro off Allenby and I get up and go with them. Outside in the semi-blackout there are three street fights in progress and all of them involve foreign volunteers. We stop and calmly watch the nearest one. A South African has a bloody nose and is struggling to rise from the curbside. He uses outrageous language which is apparently directed toward his adversary, a large soldier who is standing in the middle of the street. The sidewalks are jammed with people and many are urging on one or the other of the combatants. I look out at the soldier in the road. He is standing on the same spot where the body had lain in June.

The bistro is full and after an hour of drinking at the bar, Jake and Lev go somewhere else and I go over to a table and sit with Sol Rosen, Esther and Rachel. Rosen is a likeable American volunteer who is attached to the Yarkon motor pool and Esther and Rachel are army girls. They work at Headquarters also. Both girls are attractive and dark and Esther has grey eyes. They smile when I pull up a chair. Another hour of drinks and laughter and then we go up to Ben Yehuda and patronize the Yarden bar until after midnight. The girls have to go back to their quarters in the suburb of Montefiore and we wait with them in front of the Yarden until they get a ride in a jeep that is already full of people. We laugh and shake hands and then the jeep speeds down the street. Sol and I go back into the bar and drink until it closes.

It is early afternoon when I wake up on the couch in Sol's flat behind Shahar Street. I am alone in the room and I have a headache from the cognac and a pain over my right eye that aspirin doesn't touch. The flat is small. I go to the basin and wash and try to brush the wrinkles from my khakis. Sunlight is coming through the partly-closed blinds on the single window and I look out at the small garden below for a moment. I remember that I should be back at Herzliya but Sid Cohen had taken over as acting CO from Maury Mann and I don't worry about it for now. I leave the flat and go down the dim narrow stairs to the bright street and, when I am halfway down the block, I see Sol coming from the direction of the Yarkon. He is smiling and looks fresh and when he comes up to me on the walkway he says he is off duty for the day. He had been down at the motor pool since sunrise and now he laughs when I look at him. He has a pleasant face and a rather large nose and when he talks he has an entertaining personality. He says the girls are off duty too and they want us to join them for food and drink. We walk over a few streets and go way up to the far end of Allenby and meet Rachel and Esther at a sidewalk cafe. We sit in the shade of the trees that shelter the open section and we eat some pickled fish and drink beer. The holiday spirit continues. A party develops in a bistro across the street and we go over. We don't see anyone from the Squadron all day. When we are leaving the cafe at dusk, Dov Ben Zvi drives past. We shout at him but he maneuvers the jeep fiercely down the middle of Allenby and doesn't look to either side. We laugh.

Night falls and we are at the Gallim Yam. We had walked down along the sea wall and we could barely hear the breakers because there was so much noise on the beach road. At the Gallim Yam we have a table in the center of the open area and everyone around us is crowded together. Sol is saying something funny and the girls are laughing. They are sabras and they don't always understand Sol's humor but they laugh anyway. The evening is mild and the sea smell is good and everyone is in high spirits. Three tables away someone spills a drink on a girl's dress and a fight starts. Two volunteers lunge across the congested space and one of them falls onto Esther's lap. The volunteer grabs Esther's skirt to steady himself and she ejects him onto the floor and then everyone in the vicinity becomes engaged in the dispute. Chairs crash downward. The MPs arrive.

The Military Police section at the Yarkon takes up the entire west side of the basement area and when Sol and I and five others from the Gallim Yam arrive under escort the place is crowded. The main orderly room is busy and contains both those who are assigned there and those who have been arrested. In an adjoining room are more people behind bars in a large cell. The most interesting fact that one noticed upon entering was that everyone was arguing. Hebrew and English are being shouted at the same time and we laugh and sit down on some orange crates along the wall of the orderly room. We have lost our animosity toward the other volunteers who were brought in with us and Sol touches his swollen lip. We wait. One of the sabra MPs says we are all charged with disorderly conduct. I look at the floor and have a great desire to go back to the Gallim Yam. A half hour goes by while we watch the activity and then a Provost Marshal comes over to where we are sitting and hands us back our Service identification cards. The Provost Marshal has thinning hair and two front teeth missing from both rows. He says the disorderly conduct charges have been dropped and that all but two of us can go. He smiles and points to me and another volunteer and says we have been reported absent from our units and that we will have to remain in custody and see the military court. I have had too many drinks to be surprised and I sit back down on the orange crate and tell Sol to call Sid Cohen for me.

The military detention barracks in Jaffa had seen similar use with the British during the Mandate and, when the lorry arrives there from the Yarkon, it is three o'clock in the morning. One of the MPs helps me down from the back of the truck and we follow the others to the narrow barbed-wire gate which is the entrance. The drink is wearing off and the mounting annoyance that I am beginning to feel is only surpassed by a craving for sleep. There is an army guard at the gate and he swings it open and we pass through into the compound. There are five others in the group and we stop near the sentry post while the MPs talk with the guard. I don't know anyone who is with me although most of them are foreign volunteers. It is dark but the dirty, whitewashed walls which surround the large courtyard are quite visible as are the two low buildings which form a semi-rectangle about the open space. A light is showing from a room in an extension of one of the buildings that is nearest the gate. We soon learn that this is the Commandant's office.

Morning comes and I have slept for two hours. There is movement around me and I hear voices. I am lying on a pallet in a room of one of the low buildings. There are many more pallets and I am reminded momentarily of the long ago hostel in Haifa. I sit up. The flies are here also. I look around. The walls are bare and white and the two windows in the room are screenless. The entrance has no door. People are sitting and standing in numerous poses, dressed and undressed. Someone stops on the narrow aisle in front of the pallet. I look at the desert shoes for a second and then I look up at the face. It is Jake. He sits at the end of the pallet and laughs when I tell him what happened. He says he has been here since the first night in Tel Aviv. He is charged with assaulting an army major. He laughs again and shrugs. He says he didn't know that the chap was a major because he wasn't displaying any rank.

Outside they are serving breakfast from a table under the red-tiled overhanging roof that creates a corridor along the edge of the buildings. We stand in line and take the tea, bread and hard boiled eggs. I give mine to Jake. I keep the tea and sip from the tin cup and we go over and sit against the north wall. It is too early for the sun to reach into the courtyard and a certain coolness in the air is a sign that it is autumn. Jake looks up at the strands of barbed-wire on the top of the wall and smiles. He says that there is word that the upper echelon at Headquarters has ordered a harder line on military offenders. They think the foreign volunteers are particularly undisciplined. He throws the remainder of his tea on the ground and we laugh. I expect to be out of here by evening time.

Slender and tough, Jake has a philosophical attitude which I am well advised to initiate as the day passes. I hear nothing from the Squadron. The irritation at being in the detention compound is tempered by the fact that many of the occupants are straight out of the pages of a novel and there is a camaraderie here which makes it seem as though one is a member of a family. I walk through the yard with Jake after the meal and we talk with some of the others.

The Egyptian. Suave, even in dirty khakis, the one called the Egyptian is a Jew who was born in Cairo and he was in the Givati

Brigade. He had lost the middle finger of his right hand and he liked to say he had been wounded, but everyone laughs and says he had the finger amputated after he was stung by a scorpion. He has smooth, black hair which he slicks back. He is charged with confiscating a jeep in Tel Aviv.

The Mascot. Happy natured and pathetically trusting, the Mascot is fourteen years old. His entire family had died in the death camps of eastern Europe and how he escaped to the West no one really knew because he was fond of exaggerating. It was known that he had been adopted by a unit of US infantry and he had lived with the troops for three years and spoke English with an American accent. No one was sure how he got to Israel but he was apprehended when he tried to join the Palmach and sent to the barracks in Jaffa until it could be decided what to do with him.

Asher Ginsberg. Muscular, balding, keeping his thoughts to himself and always giving half his food to the Mascot. He was said to have been with the Stern Gang and the reason for his presence at the Jaffa barracks was obscure. No one asked any questions.

Stahl. A skinny German Jew, Stahl had miraculously escaped the death camps also but he was forever cheerful and he had an inexhaustable supply of Yiddish jokes which he recited at every opportunity.

The Italian. Small and fair-haired, the Italian spoke only his native tongue and was thus faced with a considerable conversation barrier at the compound. What little had been learned about him was almost ludicrous. He had been a fighter pilot with Mussolini's air force in World War II and had served against many of us when he was stationed in the Western Desert and Cyrenaica. He had journeyed to Israel by some devious and uncertain route without any official papers and, not only did he fail to join the Israeli Air Force, he was actually suspected as a spy initially. He had been picked up by the Military Police, penniless and singing operatic arias on a street corner in Tel Aviv. He has no charges against him but is waiting at Jaffa for a disposition on whether he will even remain in Israel. The Italian is a Christian and he has a good singing voice and in the evenings he sometimes stands at the entrance to the barrack room and entertains us with his talent.

Stahl, who is here for pilfering supplies from an army unit other than his own, points to a figure sitting alone near the wall of the south barracks. The figure wears a yarmulke and he is young and is the one everybody refers to as the Rabbi. He is in reality a fanatical religious student and now, in the midst of the holy days, he does nothing but seek solitude for the rituals that he performs with seemingly endless fervor. He has been remanded to custody for allowing his prayer practices to interfere with his military duty. The day of Yom Kippur is a half week away.

The next day I walk down to the gate with Jake. It is mid-morning and beyond the walls of the compound the sun is shining on the buildings of Jaffa. Most of them are deserted, the vacant windows staring silently at other vacant windows in a place of ghosts. Some of the facilities, like the detention barracks, are being utilized by the Israelis but for now the departure of its inhabitants from this Palestinian Arab city has left it with an aura of surrealism. We pass the Commandant's hut and he is standing on the steps. He is short and wears glasses and is good humored and sympathetic toward those who are temporarily under his control. He served with the Mandate Postal Service and he always answers questions by saying 'wait and see'. We walk on and stop at the gate and Dov comes over. Dov is the tall, blond sabra guard who has the sentry duty at the gate during the day. He also brings us the news from the outside. He speaks in Hebrew to Jake and searches in his shirt pocket for something. He has difficulty finding the article and gives Jake his Mauser while he continues searching with both hands.

By the third day at Jaffa I am beginning to believe that the Squadron doesn't know where I am. I have still heard nothing. I am lying on the pallet in the barracks room in the afternoon and others are also lying about when Jake comes through the entrance. He has heard something at the gate. He has heard that the truce has been broken. The war has started again.

It is five more days before I am exonerated of the absent without leave charge by a military board at the Yarkon. They were to be days of decision and of unqualified military successes for Israel. The Givati and Negev Brigades had launched an all-out push against the Egyptians at Isdud and actions were initiated to secure the Jerusalem sector and the roads along the disputed areas in the Tel Aviv-Jerusalem corridor. The salient and Galil fronts were comparatively quiet. 101 Squadron was to carry the bulk of the air support role in the offensive and the new Spitfires were to see their first operations. Moddy and Boris had been returned from Rhodes, unfortunately without the needed aircraft. Moddy was back at Herzliya. The last act had begun.

On the second night of the renewed fighting there is an air raid alert and we all go out into the yard of the compound and watch. Anti-aircraft tracers are sailing into the night sky from both the Jaffa and Tel Aviv areas and, between lulls in the firing, we can faintly hear the sound of engines in the air. We don't hear any bombs falling nor do we feel the earth shake from any hits. After a while there is silence and all-clear sirens wail. We go back to the barracks. In the morning Dov tells us that it was an Egyptian Dakota that was approaching Tel Aviv. Then it had turned around and decided to drop its bombs south of Rehovot. Dov has steel-rimmed glasses and he takes them off and cleans them. He says 50 chickens were killed on a kibbutz.

At the Jaffa detention barracks, Yom Kippur dawns quietly. The fasting goes on and we wait for news of the actions and I sense a strong impatience at being away from the Squadron. It is mid-October. More news of the air operations has filtered in to us. A C-46, escorted by four Messerschmitts, had bombed Gaza and Majdal the previous day and the three new Spitfires struck the base at El Arish. The Egyptians were withdrawing from Isdud. It was joyous and gratifying news but still it was difficult to curb my restlessness. That night after the end of the fast I am down by the gate with Jake and a few of the others. An army jeep has stopped outside the entrance and the two soldiers in it are talking through the wire to the night sentry. The Hebrew words are spoken loudly and Jake listens. Others go up to the wire but Jake takes my arm and we walk over toward the north wall. Jake looks at me. He says Moddy was killed at Herzliya.

In the days that followed, various versions of the crash that killed Moddy were heard but perhaps the account of Ezer, who flew as Moddy's wingman on that last mission, can throw the most light on the events leading up to the fatal accident. With the Egyptian retreat from Isdud starting to resemble a rout, Air Command had ordered the fighters to keep continual pressure on the southward-fleeing forces during the daylight hours. Sorties were flown out of Herzliya all day on Yom Kippur and, as evening approached, Moddy decided personally to take one more flight and he selected Ezer to go with him. The Messerschmitts available at that moment were 114 and the rebuilt 121. Moddy wanted 114, ostensibly because it was considered the best-rigged of all the Messerschmitts but also because the one-legged, nearly disastrous crash-landing of 121 was still fresh in his memory. Undaunted, the agreeable Ezer hopped into 121 and Moddy led out. They look off and stayed low, flying down the coast and turning in across the flats north of Majdal. Both machines were carrying bombs which they dropped on targets along the road out of Isdud. They then began to strafe the road with their guns and Ezer proceeded all the way down to Majdal. The weather was clear but they lost visual contact and, when he was out of ammunition, Ezer turned for home. His inter-plane R/T reception was faulty so he didn't bother with it and continued north. He still couldn't spot Moddy's aircraft. It was Saturday night and he made a detour to fly over the rooftop of his uncle's home in Rehovot as an impulsive triumphant gesture. As soon as he neared Herzliya he saw the tower of black smoke in the evening air and somehow he instinctively knew that Moddy had been killed. Ezer came around into the strip and landed. He had no trouble with 121.

Number 114 had crashed in an open field just south of Herzliya. The machine was destroyed and Moddy was killed instantly. There was no indication that the aircraft has been hit by return fire on the mission. One of the groundcrew at the scene has best described the real reason for the tragedy with a succinct observation. Hydraulic failure. When the undercarriage refused to lock down, Moddy had applied the centrifugal force solution. He was at 2,500 feet when the Messerschmitt went into a power spin. It was over. All Israel lamented the loss of Moddy Alon because he was a national hero – and a hero he had died on Yom Kippur. Strangely, he was the only accidental airborne fatality claimed by the Desert Hawks.

The morning sun rises brightly over the Jaffa compound but the searing heat of summer is gone. We wash our clothes at the yard trough and by the time they are dry the lorry from Yarkon is outside the barbed-wire gate. I say goodbye to the detention barracks. The Commandant hands me the order from Headquarters which dissolves the charge and returns me to duty. Jake walks with me to the barrier and Dov swings it open. I feel a certain sadness at leaving those whom I had met at Jaffa. Jake smiles when I get into the lorry and he lifts his hand in a salute. Before the week ends he will be sent to a punishment garrison at Acre.

I report to the Yarkon and prepare to go back to the Squadron. Much has changed in the time I have been away. Sid Cohen is now CO of 101 and when I see Cyril Horowitz in one of the hallways at Headquarters he says there are some new pilots at Herzliya. The Czechs have sold a whole squadron of their well-preserved Spitfire 9s to Israel and four Gentile volunteers are settled at Kafr Shmaryahu. Cyril says that the days of the Messerschmitts are numbered.

The death of Moddy seemed to have drawn the curtain on the early era. In wartime, weeks endure as months and the distant days of June and the dusty summer and the time of the Squadron pioneers were fading rapidly into the past. By November the unloved Desert Hawks were to be withdrawn from service in favor of the popular and now abundant Spitfires. It was sometimes said, by those who thought about it, that it was odd that Moddy and the Messerschmitts had passed on together. But others said, or maybe thought, that this was altogether appropriate. Their destinies had seemed intertwined since the first weeks of the conflict. The Messerschmitts had been there when it was essential that they be there and so had Moddy Alon been there. Together they had fought and defeated the enemy and now their service to Israel had ended.

CHAPTER IX

WINTER OF VICTORY

I never returned to Herzliya. That afternoon, at the Yarkon, the vision in my right eye fails again as I am walking to the motor pool to get a ride to the Squadron. This time it cannot be concealed. An orderly helps me to the Yarkon infirmary and Cyril is called down. After an examination by the Flight Surgeon I am sent out to Hadassah. There is another examination at the military hospital and the eye is bandaged to keep out the light. I am grounded and placed on detachment duty with Headquarters fighter operations which, in fact, meant that my flying days with the Israeli Air Force were over. Hadassah is out near the Yarkon River and I remain at the hospital two weeks. The chief surgeon is curious about the original head wound that caused the affliction but nothing is attempted clinically on the eye except for the daily inspection and a change of bandage each morning. The sight is returning at a slower rate and, at the end of the second week, it is decided to send me up to Haifa to a specialist. Some of the wounded from the southern fighting are coming into the hospital at intervals but they are all army and there is no one I recognize.

Leave has been cancelled at Herzliya and I don't see anyone from the Squadron either but, during my last day at Hadassah, Sol Rosen comes out to visit me and he has Esther and Rachel with him. We go outside where there are benches beneath a row of eucalyptus trees and we sit in the shade of the leaves and talk. We laugh about everything at first and then Sol is serious. He says that Stan Andrews was shot down by ground fire near Majdal. His remains were found in the wreckage of the Beaufighter by a Palmach patrol. Sol lights a cigarette. He says that Sam Pomeranz was also killed when he flew one of the recently acquired Spitfires into the side of a mountain in Yugoslavia during a storm. The girls are looking past the trees toward the river. Esther says that she used to come out here when she was ten years old and they would visit the British War Memorial and sometimes they would walk down the river bank to the beach and spend the whole day on the sand, collecting sea shells.

I leave for Haifa the next morning. During the day I go to the Yarkon and Sid Cohen brings the rest of my kit in from Herzliya. We have only a little time because he has a meeting with Aharon Remez. Sid is wearing one of the new peaked caps that have been lately issued but otherwise his appearance hasn't changed. He smiles and grasps my hand and neither of us say much. We stand next to the kit inside the main entrance of the Yarkon. Someone passing bumps Sid's shoulder but he ignores it. He says we don't have time for a drink. Maybe in the next war. We both smile and then he turns and goes into the crowd at the stairway.

It is dusk when we board the Rapide hospital plane at Sde Dov. Some of us wear sweaters because now the night breeze from the sea is chilly. I look down toward Tel Aviv and in the fading light I see the shadow-like form of the LST for the last time.

At Hadar hak Karmel I am eventually released by Haganah and returned to the States. There was, however, one more chapter to be written by 101 Squadron in Israel's War of Independence.

The assaults by Israeli forces, especially against the Egyptians, continued into the winter of 1948. The long period of containment had ended for the Jews and now the enemy was being pushed back to the Sinai. The offensive achievements of the Givati and Negev Brigades had led them to the very gates of El Arish. The situation that had prevailed in May had been reversed and, historically, it was the first Israeli thrust into the Sinai. The proceeding battles had cleared Isdud and Majdal and Gaza, as well as inland Negev positions, of enemy concentrations. As a result, the forward bases which had been evacuated in the earlier months were again put into service. 101 Squadron moved down to Hatzor, which had been shelled periodically for six months by the Egyptians in Isdud, and began operations aimed at harassing the Arab rearguard on the Sinai border. The B-17s, still operating from Ramat David, had participated in some destructive raids during this southward push and had particularly bestowed havoc on targets in what was known as the Faluja Pocket or 'bend', east of Majdal, and at Gaza where many of the Egyptian supplies were destroyed. Enemy air opposition during this time had been negligible to the point of being invisible but their anti-aircraft defenses were another matter, and could at times be deadly. The Israeli Air Force in general had been greatly strengthened by now with additional aircraft and personnel and, during the months of November and December, they roamed freely above the sands of the Sinai.

By late December only the disorganized Egyptian army, and the countless wretched Arab refugees who followed in its wake, lay between the Israelis and the Suez Canal. At this point, the British, who still maintained a sizeable force in the Canal Zone, acted under the nine-year-old Anglo-Egyptian Treaty and presented the Israel Government with an ultimatum ordering them to halt their advance into the Sinai. This was followed by a similar order from the UN and, at the same time, the

United States applied certain political pressures in an effort to persuade the Jewish leaders to comply with the ultimatum. Facing this awesome combination of diplomatic and military power, the Israelis stopped their pursuit of the Egyptians and withdrew to the Sinai border. To the credit of Dr Bunche, the UN Mediator who had been laboring diligently if unsuccessfully since October to enforce another ceasefire and settle the war peacefully, an armistice agreement was now accepted by all the belligerents which would become effective during the first week of the new year. It was to be an armistice, not another of the endless ceasefires that had stretched across the summer months, and it was to mean, in effect, an end of what would become known in Israel as the War of Independence. It was to produce a mixture of joy and frustration for the Israelis.

The original Partition boundaries were now unmistakeably secure for the Jews but many claims and counter claims that had been at issue for so long were left unresolved. Jerusalem; Samaria and Judea in the salient West Bank, places with untold religious significance for the Jews. The creation of the Gaza Strip which would point straight at Tel Aviv. The Golan Heights, where the Syrians would continue to look down on the Jewish farm settlements. The Israeli military had grave forebodings but the Armistice meant a beginning. The new State had survived its birth and now it would have time to grow strong. The Armistice became a fact on 7 January 1949.

At Hatzor, 101 Squadron welcomed the overcast winter dawn of 7 January by despatching Spitfire patrols to Abu Ageila in the Sinai where one of the largest of the Egyptian forces had halted. The armistice was not officially in force until two o'clock in the afternoon. It was meanwhile developing across the desolate expanse of the southern desert that the British, apparently to verify compliance with the earlier ultimatum, were sending out their own RAF patrols and some of these aircraft began to violate what the Jews considered Israeli airspace. An unavoidable collision course was set.

The opening clash occurred at mid-morning when six [in fact, four] Canal-based Spitfires of the RAF's 208 Squadron flew over Israeli territory in the vicinity of the El Auga-Beersheba road and then turned west and continued in the direction of the Rafah border area. Mistaking them for Egyptian aircraft, Israeli ground gunners fired at them without result. Over Rafah one of the British planes was then hit by a barrage from the Egyptians who mistook them for Israeli fighters and the pilot of the stricken machine parachuted out. Simultaneously, the remainder of the RAF flight was pounced upon from above by Spitfires of 101 Squadron. In the ensuing, and undoubtedly confusing, fight between the opposing Spitfire forces, two more [in fact, all three] of the British aircraft were shot down, one of which crash-landed behind the Egyptian front. The Israeli Spitfires in this instance were piloted by foreign

volunteers and their report of the action when they landed back at
Hatzor, while providing excitement for the rest of the Squadron
members, was met with apprehension and anxiety at Headquarters. A
retaliation by the British at this stage was a thought not to be pondered.
The bizarre chain of events continued.

Sid Cohen was in Tel Aviv for a staff meeting and it left 101 under the
joint control of Rudy Augarten, who was now Deputy Commander, and
the new Operations Officer, Ezer Weizman. Ezer was extremely anxious
to get into the air because, although he had seen more combat operations
than most during 1948, an aerial victory had been denied him. The time
was approaching noon. By 1230, Ezer and Sandy were aloft and though
they toured the Abu Ageila-El Arish area for an hour, accompanied by
two of the volunteers, they saw no other aircraft. As soon as his aircraft
has been refuelled, Ezer wanted to go out again but Headquarters was on
the Ops telephone, urging caution. While conceding that it was essential
to defend Israeli airspace, they hinted that it would be unwise 'to twist
the lion's tail too hard'. Two o'clock arrived and the armistice was now
in effect. The last airborne flight landed and made their report. An
Egyptian Fiat fighter [in fact, a Macchi MC205V] which had strayed
northward had been downed by a volunteer pilot. In frustration, Ezer ran
to the telephone and contacted control at Headquarters and somehow
convinced them to authorize another sortie over El Arish to, as Ezer
termed it, 'put on a final show of air strength'.

The British were continuing to send forth aircraft from the Canal area
in an attempt to ascertain the fate of their missing fighters and this was
probably the mission in which they were engaged when eight [in fact,
four] of the RAF Spitfires [plus 15 RAF Tempests] encountered Ezer's
flight of four over the Sinai border at 45 minutes past two o'clock. The
weather was not considered good. It was cold and generally bleak and
there were cloud formations across the entire front. In the cockpit of the
Israeli Spitfire, which was minus the canopy, Ezer sat bundled in a heavy
jacket and he wore fur-lined gloves, but he was still cold and
occasionally he shivered inadvertently. The Sinai boundary was 10,000
feet below when he saw the British machines flying north-west into
Israeli airspace. When they passed beneath the Israeli aircraft, he did not
hesitate. He rolled the Spitfire over and went straight down through the
other formation. Because of this brash maneuver, one of the foreign
volunteers managed immediately to bring down the startled Englishman
[a Tempest] who was flying at the tail end of the first British section.
This machine fell near Rafah and while Ezer regained some of his lost
height, the other planes became scattered across the sky. Disdaining the
fact that he now found himself alone with two of the unfriendly
Britishers, Ezer advanced the throttle on his Spitfire and singled out one
of the adversaries. The other plane turned quickly and Ezer saw the
cloud layers whirl around and become upside down. The British Spitfire

[in fact, it was a Tempest] was diving away and Ezer, staring through the gunsight, fired his cannon. To his surprise, spurts of vapor began to emerge from the engine of the machine in front of him and the aircraft began to fall earthward like a leaf in the wind. It grew smaller and smaller and then disappeared into a cloud. It was later reported [incorrectly] that this plane had to force-land on the base at El Arish. Ezer had his triumph in the air. He had righteously defended Israeli airspace and won. The fact that his opponent had been an RAF Spitfire [*sic*] and that the war had been officially over for an hour didn't seem to dismay him in the least. The largest victory party in the brief history of the Squadron was held that night at the Park Hotel in Tel Aviv. Ezer Weizman was master of ceremonies.

The subsequent reactions of the British to that day were at once ominous and threatening but, by the following week, Israel had been absolved by a UN investigation of the incidents of provoking the events. The British pilots who had been interned by the Israelis during the affair were returned to the RAF and the repercussions diminished and died.

There were, undoubtedly, many in the State of Israel who found significance and irony in this skirmish with the British Empire on the last day of the War of Independence. No Israeli planes had been downed in the actions. During operations 101 Squadron had accounted for 22 Arab or otherwise hostile aircraft. Not a single fighter machine was lost to the enemy in aerial combat.

The foreign volunteers drifted away one by one. In the spring of that new year [1949] the contingents of Israeli air cadets who had been training abroad would return to expand the ranks. They were young and of the future and they would see a different era. The job that the combat veterans had come to do was finished and now they drifted away. Israel would be grateful and record their deeds but now they were leaving and Israel must turn to the present and self reliance. The volunteers left as they had arrived, unheralded. There were no military bands, no medals, no uniforms, no rank. Their accomplishments wouldn't be praised or even mentioned in the annals of modern warfare. Some had died, most had survived, but the ultimate nobility lay in having served. They served in a period of desperate need at the re-birth of an ancient nation which had been waiting to be born again for twenty centuries. A homeland for the Jews. Time was to confirm that they served in a moment of history the world would never forget. Like the Desert Hawks, they served when none other was there to serve in their place. They were volunteers.

APPENDIX I

SECRET   "FORM I"

INTELLIGENCE AND PERSONAL COMBAT REPORT.

P/O. L.S. NOMIS (AMERICAN).

Date.	(A)	11/1/42.
Squadron.	(B)	71 (Eagle) Squadron.
Type of our aircraft.	(C)	Spitfire VB.
Time attack was delivered.	(D)	About 0950 hours.
Place of attack or target.	(E)	About 50 miles East of Lowestoft.
Weather.	(F)	10/10ths cloud at 11,000 feet.
Our casualties Aircraft.	(G)	Nil.
Personnel.	(H)	Nil.
Enemy casualties in air combat.	(J)	1 JU88 damaged by P/O. Nomis (American).
Enemy casualties - ground or sea targets.	(K)	N/A.

General Report.

　　　　Two Spitfires VB, Red section, 71 (Eagle) Squadron were
airborne Martlesham Heath 0910 hours, 11/1/42, with orders to scramble
base at 8,000 feet. Several Vectors were given by the Controller (F/Lt.
Cooper) and the section became separated in cloud. After receiving
several Vectors from the Controller Red 11 P/O. L.S.Nomis (American)
(Spitfire VB) found himself well out to sea and turned for home flying
at 12,000 feet. He saw a JU88 break through 10/10ths. cloud at 11,000
feet about 600 yards away to the starboard. He immediately attacked it
from the beam to the starboard quarter firing two 2½ seconds bursts with
his machine guns, opening at 300 yards and closing at 50 yards. Pieces
fell off the starboard wing of the JU88. P/O Nomis then directed his
fire towards the cockpit of the JU88 and saw some of his bullets hitting
the hood. Almost immediately the enemy aircraft dived into cloud cover
and was not seen again. The JU88 is claimed as damaged. The combat
took place about 50 miles East of Lowestoft.

　　　　Two Spitfires landed Martlesham by 1010 hours.

　　　　Our casualties.   Nil.

　　　　Enemy casualties. One JU88 damaged by P/O. Nomis
　　　　　　　　　　　　　　　　　　　　　　　　(American).

L.S. Nomis

Pilot Officer,
No. 71 (Eagle) Squadron, RAF.

Roland Robinson

Flying Officer,
Intelligence   Officer,
No. 71 (Eagle) Squadron, Royal Air Force

Secret.

Personal Combat Report. ~~Set 2~~ *Personal*

P/O. L.S. Nomis (American). ~~Set 3~~ W/C Tactics *from SP20 eastern*

Date.	(A)	17/4/42.
Unit.	(B)	71 (Eagle) Squadron.
Type and mark of our aircraft.	(C)	Spitfire VB.
Place of attack.	(D)	About 8 miles East of Felixstowe.
Time attack was delivered.	(E)	About 0715 hours.
Weather.	(F)	Clear.
Our casualties (aircraft).	(G)	Nil.
Our casualties.	(H)	Nil.
Enemy casualties in air combat.	(J)	1 Ju 88 destroyed. (Shared with P/O. J.J. Lynch (American).
Enemy casualties - ground targets	(K)	Nil.

IIN 42/d 13/4

- 106

General Report.

I took off with P/O. Lynch with orders to patrol convoy off Felixstowe. After being on patrol for about ten minutes we heard some mention of a bogie on the R/T and we proceeded out to sea to see if we could find anything. After about 15 minutes I observed an aircraft coming up very fast to our port beam at our same altitude, which was nought feet. This proved to be a Ju 88. P/O. Lynch and myself were flying fairly close line abreast and we saw the 88 at about the same time he saw us. The 88 made a hard right turn upon seeing us and we made a hard left turn to attack. The 88 levelled off and made off at top speed, altering his course about 45 degrees to either side every so often. P/O. Lynch and myself were coming up astern of the 88, he Lynch being slightly ahead and above as he was nearest to the 88 when we turned. I saw P/O. Lynch fire a burst which was slightly out of range as it hit in the water behind the 88's tail. I then fired one burst from directly astern, and this too hit behind the tail. I decided not to fire again until I was closer up. During this time I was closing up both on P/O. Lynch and the 88, and when I was about 50 yards behind P/O. Lynch and below he being about 200 yards behind the 88, I saw black smoke coming out of Lynch's engine. This increased in volume as I was watching and he suddenly pulled up and away to port, saying on the R/T that he had been hit. That was the last I saw of him as all my attention was on the 88. All this time I was closing on the 88, making quarter attacks from astern and beam and changing my position all the time from port to astern to starboard as I was receiving fairly accurate return fire from the top rear gunner. I observed strikes on the wings, fusilage and tail of the 88 and on my next to last attack the gunner did not fire, that is, stopped firing and did not fire at all on my last attack during which I ran out of ammunition.

My last three attacks were with machine guns alone as I had used up all my cannons. My last attack was from abeam and above at a fairly steep angle and I observed strikes in the fusilage and starboard wing. I closed to about 50 yards and broke away to the left and above upon running out of ammunition.

I then turned my aircraft around in time to see the 88 emit a billow of (an explosion and) black smoke and plunge into the sea. Upon climbing my plane to observe the spot I could see a great disturbance and wake on the water but no sign of the aircraft or occupants. I then reported this on th R/T and turned for home on a reciprocal until I got a direct vector from the controller.

L.S. Nomis

Pilot Officer,
No. 71 (Eagle) Squadron,
Martlesham Heath.

APPENDIX II

DELIVERY SCHEDULE
OF AVIA S-199s FROM CZECHOSLOVAKIA TO ISRAEL

Balak	Delivery	Aircraft	Date of Arrival	Comments
5	C-54	NC58021	20/5/48	
7	C-46		21/5/48	
9	C-54	NC58021	22/5/48	
11	C-46	RX-136	24/5/48	Crashed on arrival, Avia destroyed.
12	C-46		25/5/48	
13	C-46		25/5/48	
16	C-46		30/5/48	
18	C-54		30/5/48	
19	C-46		31/5/48	
20	C-46		31/5/48	
51	C-46	RX-133	1/7/48	
52	C-46	RX-138	?1/7/48	
55	C-46	RX-133	?4/7/48	
54	C-46	RX-134	7/7/48	Delayed in Yugoslavia for four days.
58	C-46	RX-135	9/7/48	
60	C-46	RX-138	13/7/48	
62	C-54	NC58021	14/7/48	
63	C-54		?15/7/48	
65	C-46	RX-134	11/48	Emergency landing at Rome airport 18/7/48; departure delayed until November 1948
66	C-46	RX-135	?17/7/48	
67	C-46	RX-130	19/7/48	
68	C-54	NC56011	18/7/48	
70	C-46	RX-138	20/7/48	
76	C-54		24/7/48	
79	C-54	RX-121	28/7/48	

APPENDIX III

RECORD OF LEO NOMIS' KNOWN S-199 FLIGHTS IN ISRAEL

IDF/AF archival records, from which the following basic details were extracted, suggest that Leo Nomis flew a total of 10.50 hours on the S-199 while in Israel, but this is clearly incorrect.

Date	Aircraft No	Times	Comments
6/8/48	108	1535-1615	Training flight
7/8/48	120	1501-1551	Training flight
8/8/48	108	1203-1245	Training flight
9/8/48	121	1540-1617	Operational patrol; intercepted UN Dakota carrying Count Bernadotte.
13/8/48	115	1715-1758	Operational patrol, searching for reconnaissance aircraft. Sighted RAF Mosquito but unable to intercept.
16/8/48	114	1302-1330	Operational patrol
20/8/48	115	1220-1323	Operational patrol
24/8/48	114	1245-1355	Operational patrol; returned early due to engine malfunction.
5/9/48	121	1140-1310	Operational patrol; damaged in landing accident on return to Herzliya.*
7/9/48	122	1125-1246	Operational patrol
11/9/48	118	1150-1209	Operational patrol; returned early due to engine malfunction.

* During the course of this patrol Leo sighted an RAF photographic-reconnaissance Mosquito from 13 Squadron, at which he fired, believing the shufti kite to have been an Iraqi aircraft:

'I came close enough to fire a burst at long range. The Mosquito then entered a long bank of clouds and contact was lost. After I reported to the IO we talked for a while about confirming something in the matter of time and place, which was north of Acre. We determined that the Mosquito had probable Iraqi markings. By the end of the month nothing further had arisen so I more or less forgot about it.'

Five flights are apparently not officially recorded in IDF/AF records shown above; these are recorded in Leo's manuscript as:

1/8/48	114		First flight with 101 Squadron; duration of at least 1.15 hours (morning).
1/8/48	114		Second flight, of about 1 hour duration (afternoon).
8/8/48	113		Test flight, duration 30 minutes. On return to Natanya ground-looped without damage to aircraft.
21/9/48	?		Operational flight, searching for intruding Dragon Rapide.
3/10/48	?	1530-1645	To provide escort for Spitfires being flown to Israel from Czechoslovakia; failed to rendezvous.

In addition, Leo clocked 4.45 hours on the S-199 during the conversion course in Czechoslovakia; he also carried out three operational flights in the PR Spitfire (130) while in Israel.

APPENDIX IV

INDIVIDUAL HISTORIES OF ISRAEL's S-199s

101   Shot down by ground fire either 29/5/48 (Eddie Cohen killed) or 30/5/48 (Milton Rubenfeld baled out).

102   Shot down by ground fire either 29/5/48 (Eddie Cohen killed) or 30/5/48 (Milton Rubenfeld baled out).

103   With Maintenance Unit in late July 1948; no other details known.

104   With Maintenance Unit in late July 1948; no other details known.

105   Sustained damage by ground fire 10/6/48 (flown by Moddy Alon); with Maintenance Unit late July, no other details known.

106   Damaged in take-off accident at Herzliya June 1948 (flown by Giddy Lichtman). With Maintenance Unit late July 1948; to Maintenance Unit November 1948 for salvage.

107   Shot down by Syrian Harvard 10/7/48 (Leslie Block killed).

108   First S-199 to receive 101 Squadron badge on port engine cowling. Accident 21/8/48; accident 30/10/48, to Maintenance Unit. Repaired and renumbered 1906; transferred to Tel-Nof 1950.

109   With Maintenance Unit late July 1948; subsequently written-off.

110   Lost in action 9/7/48 (Bob Vickman killed).

111   With Maintenance Unit late July 1948, probably written-off.

112   With Maintenance Unit late July 1948, probably written-off.

113   Delivered to 101 Squadron 19/7/48; ground-looped by Leo Nomis 9/8/48 undamaged. Written-off in belly-landing accident 16/10/48 (flown by Leon Frankel).

114   Delivered to 101 Squadron 19/7/48. Leo Nomis' first Avia flight in Israel 1/8/48; Crashed near Herzliya 16/10/48 (Moddy Alon killed).

115   Delivered to 101 Squadron 20/7/48. Written-off in landing accident

at Herzliya 9/9/48 (flown by Sandy Jacobs).

116   With Maintenance Unit late July 1948; believe damaged in landing accident at Herzliya in August 1948 (flown by Cyril Horowitz). With MU in November 1948.

117   Damaged in landing accident 20/8/48 (flown by Mitchell Flint); damaged in belly-landing at Tel-Nof 17/10/48 (flown by Giddy Lichtman). To Maintenance Unit, repaired and renumbered 1901.

118   Shot down Arab Airways Dragon Rapide 23/9/48 (flown by Giddy Lichtman). Renumbered 1902 and transferred to Tel-Nof in 1950.

119   Delivered to 101 Squadron 20/7/48. Modified as PR aircraft; written-off in landing accident at Herzliya 8/10/48 (flown by Bill Pomerantz).

120   Ground-looped 14/9/48 Sflown by Bill Pomerantz). Repaired and renumbered 1903; transferred to Tel-Nof in 1950.

121   Landing accident at Herzliya 5/9/48 (flown by Leo Nomis). Shot down REAF Spitfire 16/10/48 (flown by Rudy Augarten). Renumbered 1904 and transferred to Tel-Nof in 1950.

122   Written-off in take-off accident at Herzliya 16/9/48 (flown by Cyril Horowitz).

123   Renumbered 1905. Damaged when undercarriage accidently retracted on the ground 18/2/49; repaired and transferred to Tel-Nof in 1950.

124   Delayed at Rome Airport on board C-46 RX-134 18/7/48 until November 1948. Renumbered 1907 and written-off in take-off accident 15/12/48 (flown by Wayne Peake).

NB: Unidentified Avia damaged in landing accident at Herzliya 1/8/48.

For the record: On the eve of Operation Yoav, which commenced on 15 October 1948, 101 Squadron had on strength eight operational Avia S-199s: 108, 113, 114, 117, 118, 120, 121, 123.

Research would suggest that the Avias were credited with shooting down two REAF Dakotas (by Moddy Alon); three REAF Spitfires (one each by Moddy Alon, Giddy Lichtman and Rudy Augarten); one Syrian Harvard (by Maurice Mann); and one Arab Airways Dragon Rapide (by Giddy Lichtman).

DRAMATIS PERSONNAE

Readers who have enjoyed Leo Nomis' *The Desert Hawks* are invited to read Brian Cull's *Spitfires over Israel* for further in-depth information and background to the story of his personal experiences during this conflict, which became known to Israelis as the War of Independence.

Brian Cull has written the following titles for Grub Street of London, publishers of this book.

Air War for Yugoslavia, Greece and Crete, 1940-41 with Christopher Shores and Nicola Malizia

Malta: The Hurricane Years, 1940-41 with Christopher Shores and Nicola Malizia

Malta: The Spitfire Year, 1942 with Christopher Shores and Nicola Malizia

Bloody Shambles, Volume 1 (the fall of Singapore and Dutch East Indies, 1941-42) with Christopher Shores and Yasuho Izawa

Bloody Shambles, Volume 2 with Christopher Shores and Yasuho Izawa

Twelve Days in May (Hurricane Squadrons in France, May 1940) with Bruce Lander and Heinrich Weiss

Wings over Suez (the Suez Conflict of 1956 and sequel to *Spitfires over Israel*) with David Nicolle and Shlomo Aloni

249 at War (a history of 249 Squadron, the RAF's top-scoring fighter squadron of World War II)

Amongst forthcoming titles is the eagerly-awaited two-volume study of British and Commonwealth participation in the Korean airwar of 1950-1953.